the Jazz Musician's Guide to Creative Practicing

Notes on the difficult, humorous, endless path of becoming a better improvising musician!

by

David Berkman

Includes CD

Editor and Publisher - Chuck Sher
Graphics and Cover Art - Attila Nagy
Cover Painting - Daniel Boccato
Text Editor - Bonnie Allen
© 2007 SHER MUSIC CO., P.O. Box 445, Petaluma, CA 94953
All Rights Reserved. International Copyright Secured. Made in the USA.
ISBN 1-883217-48-2

Table of Contents

CD Examples

INTRODUCTION: *One Pianist's Jazz Odyssey*

This book is about the process of learning to be an improvising musician. It's mostly about how to learn and how to practice. It's a little bit about theory, a little bit about ear training and a little bit about composition. It's a little bit country and a little bit rock and roll. (Actually, it's neither of those things). It has some stories about great musicians that I've worked with that I hope are instructive and/or entertaining. It has some jokes, which I have been told are not all equally funny. (So at this point, try to stay optimistic). This book is different from a lot of other books about jazz. It's mostly ideas about things you might try when you are practicing, but I have stayed away from giving you licks to learn. I give examples of things I've found helpful to practice, but wherever possible I urge you to try to take the idea of an exercise and alter it or come up with something on your own. I don't know what you need to practice to become a better jazz musician; no one does. I don't know what you need any more than anyone knew what Monk needed to work on when he was a young musician, or any other great musician before their voices were incorporated into the jazz tradition. I have some ideas, though, of things that could help you have more fun and get more done when you do practice. If you learn to practice well, maybe you'll have a better idea of what sort of player you want to be.

This book is concerned with problems that we all have to deal with, and each topic in the book is a sort of master class or private lesson dealing with ways to work on a problem. Musical problems are things like playing fast or spelling chord changes more clearly or making lines over complex chord progressions or playing in odd meters or learning bebop vocabulary. We start with some of the more basic problems and then work our way up to more complicated things.

The problems are pretty easy to come up with; they are the sorts of things that jazz musicians spend a lifetime practicing. Along with the sections devoted to problems, I have included practice tips that sometimes are truly practice tips and sometimes are digressions, stories or jokes. I've tried to make this book as linear and straightforward as possible, but one of the things I don't like about jazz instruction books is that they are too linear and straightforward, so I had a little trouble with that part. If you are practicing something in the main text, you can ignore the practice tips and concentrate on the specific thing that you are working on. If you are not practicing and are just reading through the book, you can read through the practice tips to get more general ideas about ways to practice, not tied to specific exercises. Most jazz method books make it sound like there is a step-by-step process through which you get better and better until you have mastered the subject of the book, whatever that is. These books usually have a lot of pages devoted to writing things out in different keys, since that takes up a lot of pages. There must be people who like these books and buy them—there are so many of them out there. Personally, I don't like these books much—they don't work for me because practicing isn't really like that, at least it isn't like that for me. I am working on things today that I should have finished a long time ago if I were proceeding in a straight line, and I will pick them up and put them down many more times, I'm afraid, before I retire to that practice cubicle in the sky.

My idea for this book is that, at the least, you can dip it into and pick up something that might help give you a new idea about the way you practice a particular thing. If you dip in several times and get a few really good ideas about ways to make your practice more enjoyable, then it will be worth the price of the book.

Of course, these ideas won't help much if you don't practice. Try to find one thing that you want to work on each time you pick up the book. Then go work on it. Or pretend we are having a lesson together, or that this book is a sort of practice coach, albeit a fairly easygoing one that never tells you to run wind sprints or drop on the floor and give it 20 pushups.

I think that students tend to be pretty uncreative about ways to practice. I think that developing a good practice method or, to put it better, becoming creative about the process of practicing, is the most important skill that jazz students need to develop. Recently a student complimented me by saying that I have a lot of discipline to practice the things I have practiced and it took me back to the time in my life when it seemed like practicing was something that required a lot of discipline. Now, I tend to think of practice as an exploration. I practice simpler things and enjoy practicing more than I ever have. I go through periods where I practice a lot and periods where I don't get to practice much. A lot of that has to do with my life, which involves a fair amount of traveling, playing, teaching and writing music, all of which eat into practice time. Sometimes I'm just not in the mood.

Recent books like Kenny Werner's "Effortless Mastery" have started to address an imbalance in jazz pedagogy (there's a frightening couple of words) by examining the thoughts and methodology of jazz students' practice lives. This book presents a somewhat different approach, although I think it is largely compatible with Kenny's thinking.

As a student, teacher and professional musician for the last 30 years or so, I work on these issues daily. I am not a prodigy, and as a non-prodigy I have had to develop my playing, my ears, my technique and rhythm through practice. I've gotten better over the years at playing and practicing.

This book is written from the perspective of a pianist. About 85 percent of the material in this book is aimed at all instrumentalists. Here and there are exercises aimed specifically at pianists. Some of the simpler piano exercises should be done by everyone, since an understanding of basic piano and keyboard harmony is extremely useful to any musician. In addition to this, for non-pianists, understanding how other instrumentalists approach music will enrich your own practice and give you ideas of new directions you want to explore on your own instrument. In the few more advanced piano-oriented sections having to do with specific piano textures (stride, multi-line playing, walking bass lines and left-hand rhythms against right-hand melodies), I would recommend that non-pianists not spend too much time and of course feel free to skip to the next relevant section.

Skipping is always allowed. I've tried to present a variety of approaches to problem solving and some of them might not be for you. They might be for someone else, so skip to the next section and see if that works better for you.

I hope you can use this book to give you ideas of things to work on, and more importantly, ways to work. Some people who read this book before it was published suggested that there are sections where I need to spell out more simply a step-by-step process for practicing a particular thing. There are many sections where I DO give you a step-by-step procedure, (especially the part of the book devoted to "Giant Steps") but sometimes I am speaking more generally, suggesting a direction that you might think about. Sometimes you have to work out the steps on your own. I don't think that's necessarily a deficiency in the book. I think many students have gotten so used to being told what to do that they haven't developed the ability to generate ideas on their own. This is especially true with the piano-oriented sections of the book. If you are a non-pianist, you can decide whether these sections are relevant to you or not.

I've been fortunate in that I've had a lot of help from some great teachers, among them Sophia Rosoff, Kenny Werner, Gaby Yaron, Charlie Banocos, Fred Hersch, Ace Carter, Bill Gidney, Bob Mover, Willy Smith, Bill Dearango, and Jeff Covell. I've learned as much from peers and I continue to do so, including: Bruce Barth, Dick Oatts, Adam Kolker, Donny McCaslin, Tony Scherr, Dave Pietro, Gerald Cleaver, Johannes Weidenmuller, Nasheet Waits and countless others. I've also been fortunate to play with some amazing jazz players (among them those I just named and many others), some famous and some not, and their contributions are here.

I've learned a lot from students, and the process of organizing my thoughts to teach something has often spurred me to practice. (I say this for the benefit of students of mine who have told me that they don't want to teach. To each his or her own of course, but you'd be surprised how much you learn from students, and from preparing things for students. Anyway, I certainly am surprised). All of these people's contributions have made their way into this book, credited when the information was traceable to something a specific person said or showed me, uncredited for the bulk of information that I have absorbed from being a part of this community of musicians.

Practicing jazz is a difficult process to get a grip on. In general, we tend to think of practicing as polishing something until we can play it perfectly and without mistakes. Improvisation seems almost the opposite: it's all about surprise—making something up that hasn't been heard before. So how do we practice that?

That is the question this book attempts to answer. My answers are based on many years as a teacher and student of the music. In the end, how you decide to practice will determine what you sound like. Deciding what and how to practice is a creative act that every musician figures out in his or her own way. Hopefully, this book will give you ideas of things to practice and ways to work that will help you to find your own unique way.

David Berkman

"I may not be the best teacher you ever had, but I am trying to become the last teacher you will ever need..."

~ Moshe Feldenkrais

"A great teacher is one who realizes that he himself is also a student and whose goal is not to dictate the answers, but to stimulate his students' creativity enough so that they go out and find the answers themselves."

~ Herbie Hancock

CHAPTER 1: *Theory Review*

What You Need to Know to Begin

For a long time I have been thinking that the most important ideas of basic jazz theory could be boiled down to 5 pages. That wasn't true, it turned out—it took 14. If you are pretty conversant with jazz theory and chord scales you can skim this part. You can always come back and review if something theoretical comes up down the line that you don't understand. I'm going to proceed pretty quickly with this part, so if you are new to music and are interested in learning beginning music theory, you'd do better with a more basic text that treats the following theory in much greater detail than we will do here. This is a quick summary of the big picture. Anyway, here goes.

The Major Scale and Its Modes

A large chunk of theory comes from the major scale and its modes. Major scales are a combination of whole and half steps: whole, whole, half, whole, whole, whole, half. There are 7 different notes in the major scale and they are assigned the numbers 1, 2, 3, 4, 5, 6, 7—the famous do, re, mi, fa, sol, la, ti of solfege classes and the *Sound of Music*.

If I tell you to play 1, 2, b3, 4, 5, 6, b7, I am describing a scale that is not a major scale because the 3rd and 7th scale degrees are flatted and so this scale does not have the pattern of whole, whole, half, whole, whole, whole, half.

As it turns out, the above scale is the same as a major scale that starts on the second degree: 2, 3, 4, 5, 6, 7, 1 (in this case Bb major). A scale that is a major scale starting on a degree other than 1 is called a mode of that major scale. So we have two ways of describing the above scale. I can tell you to play a major scale starting on the 2nd degree (a Bb major scale that goes from C to shining C) or I can tell you to play a scale that starts on C (1) and continues 2 b3 4 5 6 b7. It's important to understand both of these ways of describing the scale. I want to see that scale and think C minor, so knowing the pattern of scale degrees is very important, more important than knowing the scale as a Bb scale starting on the C.

The modes all have names and usually at this point in a theory book, you get to learn them now and this book is no exception.

1: Bb Ionian – a normal homey sort of Bb major scale

2: C Dorian – a neutral kind of C minor scale

3: D Phrygian – a darker kind of D minor scale

4: Eb Lydian – a more impressionistic (than Ionian) sort of Eb major scale

5: F Mixolydian – a plain sort of F dominant 7th scale

6: G Aeolian – a homey sort of G minor scale AKA natural minor

7: A Locrian – a half-diminished, dark A scale

Diatonic Triads and Sevenths

Okay, so far so good. Now if we build a 7th chord (4 notes stacked in thirds) using only the notes of the scale on each step, we get a series of seven different chords, called diatonic sevenths. We can also build triads (3 notes stacked in thirds) on each scale step and these are called diatonic triads. Triads come in four varieties or **qualities** (major, minor, diminished and augmented) though only major, minor and diminished triads are found in the diatonic triads of a major scale. Seventh chords come in many different qualities (depending on how you define certain chords) but only four different qualities occur in the diatonic seventh chords of the major scale (major 7ths, minor 7ths, dominant 7ths and minor 7th b5's or half diminished). The quality for each diatonic triad or 7th chord found on a particular scale degree is always the same no matter what key you are in. By this I mean that the chord built on the first degree of the scale is always a major 7th, the second is always a minor 7th, etc. Here are the diatonic 7ths or triads for the major scale:

scale degree 1: major 7th (or a major triad)
scale degree 2: minor 7th (or a minor triad)
scale degree 3: minor 7th (or a minor triad)
scale degree 4: major 7th (or a major triad)
scale degree 5: dominant 7th (or a major triad)
scale degree 6: minor 7th (or a minor triad)
scale degree 7: minor 7th b5 or half diminished 7th (or a diminished triad)

(By convention, we use roman numerals to describe these chords, upper case for major and dominants, lower case for everything else. I understand that this has changed and not everyone uses the uppercase/lower case distinction for these chords, so for those of you who don't, please bear with me).

How Chords Function

These chords are put together to make cadences—basic chord progressions. A cadence is like a sentence. Sentences have nouns, verbs and objects; and cadences have tonic, subdominant and dominant chords. The most basic cadence is I IV V I. (The most basic expression of these chords is as triads, although in jazz contexts they are more often found as seventh chords). In this cadence we begin and end with the I chord, which is called the tonic. The V chord (dominant) leads strongly toward the return of the I chord at the end of the sentence. The V chord has an unstable feeling, like we aren't going to stop there. The IV chord (subdominant) takes us away from the I chord, but we don't feel quite the same instability as we do with the V chord. We probably won't stay there but it wouldn't kill us if we did. (A quick qualification is in order. The word "instability" is a sort of analogy, a way of describing these musical sounds in words. A V7 chord isn't really "unstable" per se; it sounds like a V7 chord, although most people hearing it would probably feel that it does tend to want a resolution. You need to develop a familiarity with these sounds so that a IV chord sounds like a IV chord and a V chord sounds like a V chord to you. It's the same with the qualities I ascribed to the modes a few paragraphs back. These are subjective descriptions. An Ionian scale sounds like an Ionian scale and a Lydian like a Lydian).

The above cadence is called a full cadence because we end back at the I chord—we've come home to the tonic. We can also have a half cadence that ends on the V. We pause there at the end of a sentence, but that's only because there is another sentence coming that starts on a tonic chord. This is typical of first endings in standard songs—they leave you hanging on that V chord which then strongly encourages you to go back to the beginning of the section.

They are like questions waiting for an answer, aren't they? Yes, they are. (That was a half cadence followed by a quick full cadence).

So, what about the other numbers? We've talked about I, IV and V but what about ii, iii, vi and vii?

These other chords are coloristic variations of the I, IV and V. The vi and iii chords act like tonic chords, meaning you can replace I with vi or iii (or both if you wish), and the sentence still makes sense. (We say that these chords "function" like a tonic, which is where the phrase "functional harmony" comes from, meaning tonal music with cadences that have these chordal relationships). A ii chord acts like a subdominant, meaning it can replace IV, and vii is dominant, a substitute for the V chord. Using one of these substitutes is like changing the sentence: "My reindeer is sick" to "My wildebeest has cholera." Same basic template but the nuance is different.

So I IV V I can become I IV V vi or iii vi ii V I (I replaced the I chord with two tonic chords here to come up with this often used cadence, which jazz players call a "turnaround") or any other combination of tonic functioning chords followed by subdominant functioning chords followed by dominant functioning chords followed by tonic functioning chords. Getting used to the sound of all of the color changes available for each kind of function will give you more choices about what kind of harmony you want to use when you are arranging, composing or playing songs.

If the I IV V I is the most basic sentence in music, the more common variant of that for jazz music and standard songs is ii V7 to I.

Secondary Dominants

I'm going to repeat myself here (something you can't afford to do much if you are going to cover all of harmony in 5 or even 14 pages) to emphasize that the resolution of V7 to I is of central importance to understanding tonal harmony. The instability of the V7 chord implies the I chord that follows it. V to I is the mother of all resolutions and so it is a big deal. In fact, that's where our next group of chords come from: they are called secondary dominants and they are the dominant chords that go with each of the diatonic sevenths. For example, if I am in the key of Ab, then C-7 is the iii-7 in that key. This chord will occasionally be preceded by its dominant, G7. Now, you would expect to find Gminor7b5 in Ab, the chord built on the 7th degree of the scale, not a G7, which has notes that aren't found in an Ab major scale. But the G7 sets up the C-7. It's like a tiny modulation into another key, but it's too brief to feel like we've left the key of Ab. We've just set up the C-7 with a V to I type resolution. We call this chord the V7 of iii (and write it as V7/iii). Using secondary dominants gives us a lot more chord choices for our diatonic progressions.

It's also worth mentioning that whenever we have a secondary dominant we can precede it with the ii-7 that goes along with this V7. Sometimes these "related ii chords" will give us more chords that aren't diatonic. For example, again in the key of Ab, we can use V7/IV (Ab7) to lead to the IV chord, DbMa7. We can proceed the Ab7 with its related ii-7, Eb-7—another chord that has notes not found in the key of Ab— further enlarging our harmonic palette.

The Blues

Let's take a break from cadences and talk about something a little bit different: the blues. You know it, it's a part of American culture from "Johnny B. Good" to the theme to Batman. It's everywhere. What is it? (And don't say depression, which is also everywhere and a pretty significant feature of American culture. At jazz camps, occasionally we combine the musical and pathological meanings of the blues by teaching a few angry adolescents the blues scale, but I digress).

Blues is two different things. First, it is a form. It is a 12-bar chord progression without any major7 chords. The blues is a combination of major and minor harmony, and the tonic chords—the I chords—are all dominant 7ths. (I am speaking of the most basic blues form here. The jazz and blues tradition is filled with harmonic variations on this

that break these basic rules). That is one of its unique features and something that differentiates it from the functional harmony we were discussing earlier, which, you will no doubt notice, contained no I dominant 7th chords. Here is the basic structure:

I7 for four bars, IV7 for two bars I7 for two bars. V7 for a bar. IV7 for a bar and then I7 for a bar with something at the end to point us back toward the top (V7, right?)

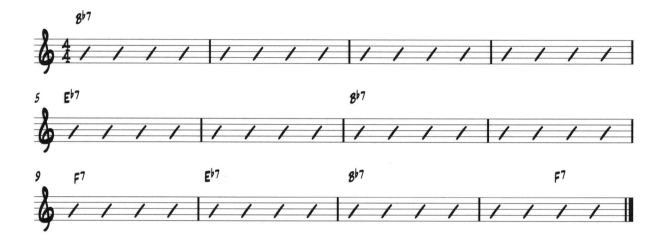

There is more that is unusual to this form than the I7 chords. It doesn't have the regular sort of V to I cadences (except in the last bar heading back up to the top) but resolves backwards from the V7 to the IV7 to the I7 (IV to I is, in classical talk, a plagal cadence— the amen chord at the end of a hymn to non-classical folks).

Secondly, blues is also a scale, a melodic sound in addition to being a harmonic form. An interesting thing about this scale is that you can play it over the whole form— meaning you don't have to change scales when you change chords. The blues scale works over every chord in the progression. The scale is 1, b3, 4, #4, 5, b7. It's a fairly simple scale but great blues players can spin endless variations from it. (Keep in mind that I am simplifying a lot here, but this is the basis for blues playing at its most basic).

So we end up with two ways to solo over the blues: we can use the blues scale or we can play the chord scales that come from the modes that we discussed earlier. More about playing chord scales later.

(I want to emphasize here that simply knowing the blues scale or any other scale for that matter only gets you started with playing the blues. All this theory only becomes art when you are really hearing it, and applying it musically, but this is a place to start).

Of course we can add chords to the blues progression. The most common variation is the bebop blues form. This form differs from the basic blues form by changing the V, IV progression in the 9th and 10th bar to a more normal functioning ii-7, V7 and by adding secondary dominants.

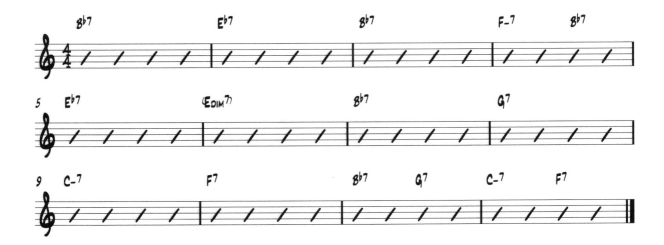

There are lots of common variations for the blues form, but these two forms, the basic blues form and the bebop blues form (with a whole lot of slight variations) are the most common. Another somewhat less common variation is the "Blues for Alice" or Bird blues form. This blues form is pretty far removed from our original basic blues form and even more like functional harmony. We get a major 7th in the first bar and a lot of added secondary dominants and their related ii chords.

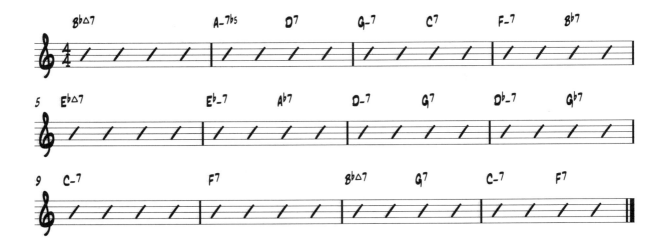

Chord Scales

Okay, we're moving along pretty well here. Having covered some blues basics and a little bit about diatonic harmony, let's talk about chord scales. At the end of the day, converting chords into scales is one of the most important topics of jazz theory. Knowing nothing at all about chord scales, you would still know 4 of the notes of any chord scale: the chord tones—1,3,5 and 7—but you need to know about the notes that come in between these. Most chord scales have seven notes so you only have 3 more notes that haven't been determined: the scale tones 2, 4 and 6. The simplest way to build chord scales is to add the 2 that is found one whole step above the root, the 4 that is found one whole step above the 3rd, and the 6th that is found one whole step above the 5th.

Using this approach, the scales below are generated, some of which we already talked about when we were discussing modes:

major 7th = 1 2 3 #4 5 6 7 (Lydian)
minor 7th = 1 2 b3 4 5 6 b7 (Dorian)
dominant 7th = 1 2 3 #4 5 6 b7 (Mixolydian #11 or Lydian b7)
minor7b5 = 1 2 b3 4 b5 b6 b7 (Locrian natural 9)
diminished 7th = 1 2 b3 4 b5 b6 bb7 natural7 (whole step/half step diminished scale)

Sure enough, all of the above scales work well over the chord types that they were derived from. The first two of the scales above are modes of the major scale and as I said, we've seen them before. The mixolydian b7 and locrian natural 9 scale are derived from another scale — the melodic minor scale. The melodic minor scale is a major scale with a flatted 3rd. (In jazz, when we talk about a melodic minor scale, we are talking about the scale that classical musicians call the "melodic minor ascending." Jazz melodic minor is the same scale going up and down). We can look at the modes of this scale just as we did with the major scale. We get some interesting scales this way, they are:

1st mode: melodic minor

2nd mode: Dorian b2

14

3rd mode: Lydian #5

4th mode: Lydian b7

5th mode: Mixolydian b6

6th mode: Locrian natural 9

7th mode: altered

All of these scales have their uses but some get used more than others. Particularly useful are the 1st mode, the melodic minor (used over minor major 7ths); the 3rd mode, the major #4,#5 scale (used over Major 7th #5 chords); the 4th mode, the Lydian b7 scale (used over dominant #11 chords); the 6th mode, Locrian Natural 9 (used over minor7 b5 chords); and the 7th mode, the altered scale (used over altered dominants—dominants that have b9, #9 b13).

The last scale that we need to look at is the scale built from the diminished 7th chord and the whole steps above each chord tone. This scale is an 8-note scale called the octotonic or diminished scale. This scale is built of alternating whole steps and half steps. There are two varieties of this scale (which are actually modes of each other): the scale that is built of alternating whole and half steps starting with a whole step (which is sometimes called the "whole/half diminished scale" or natural 9 diminished scale),

and the scale that is built of alternating whole and half steps starting with a half step (the "half/whole diminished scale" or b9 diminished scale).

The first scale is used over diminished 7th chords, the second scale is used over dominant 7ths (specifically 13 b9 #9 chords).

Chord Scale Options

You can see pretty easily that each chord quality has more than one scale that can be used with it, so there are several options for each chord quality. Choosing one or another scale is a color choice. If the chord that you are soloing over is a major 7th, for example, the Ionian scale (1234567) is an option and the Lydian scale (123#4567) is an option. The Lydian scale is a little bit more misty or impressionistic sounding. The Ionian is more homespun or square (I don't mean in the hip versus square sense of that word—I mean that it's even, straight). If I am willing to use a scale that makes the major7 into a major7#5 (a sort of more exotic variant of the major7 chord) I can include the Lydian #5 scale (123#4#567) in my chord scale options to play over a major 7th. This scale is the third mode of the melodic minor scale. In learning the scale options for each chord, it's important to develop a sense of the color differences between the scales. Of course, these color differences are subjective; everyone can find his or her own terms for what quality a particular scale has. I tend to arrange the scales on a sort of scale (okay, it's a scale scale), ranging from dark to light or mild to spicy, less altered to more altered. Here are the most common scales for each of the common chord qualities.

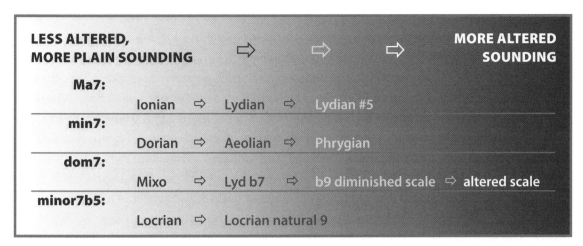

Is that everything? Well, almost. There are a few more chord scales that we haven't talked about. These include:

the whole-tone scale (used over dominant 7th #5 chords)

the minor third/half step scale (or augmented scale) used over minor major 7th chords or major 7#5 chords

the harmonic minor scale and its modes

especially the 5th mode

which is used over dominant7 b9 b13 chords.

Chord Tensions

Let's talk about tensions for a moment. Tensions (9, 11 and 13), the upper parts of chords, are usually found a whole step above the 1,3 and 5 of seventh chords, as we noted earlier. (We usually use the numbers 2, 4 and 6 when we are talking about scale degrees, and 9, 11 and 13 when we are talking about the tensions of a chord.) These notes are the available harmonic choices for each chord quality (by which I mean, the tensions that are most commonly used for each chord quality). So, the available tensions for Major 7ths are 9, #11 and 13. The available tensions for minor 7ths are 9, 11 and 13. The available tensions for minor 7thb5 chords are 9,11 and b13. the available tensions for minor major 7ths are 9, 11 and 13. The available tensions for diminished chords are located a whole step above the notes in a diminished chord. This is really just another way of getting to the scales we talked about before, focusing on what the normal available tensions are for each chord type, but we are concerned here with harmonizing the chords vertically.

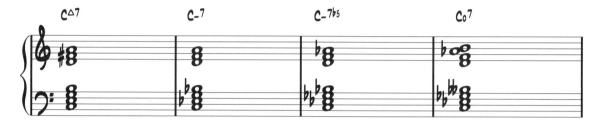

(Keep in mind that when I say that the tensions "are available," I mean that if you are going to add a 9th or 11th, the "available tension" is the sort of 9th or 11th that gets added 95 percent of the time. Also, if you are reading chord changes and you see a Major 7th, you are free to add the 9th, #11th or 13th. How good each of these tensions sounds in any particular context depends on how rich a chord you want for that specific situation). Unlike chord scales, where every chord quality had more than one scale option, when we speak of available tensions we are always referring to one set per chord quality (with the exception of the dom7sus4 chord, see below).

A few chords have tensions that are not located a whole step above the chord tones of the chord. The available tensions for a dominant7sus4 are 9, 13 and 3 or b9, b13 and b3 (one set or the other), and the available tensions for a dominant 7th are b9, 9, #9, #11, b13 and 13. Dominant 7ths have the most choices, and becoming familiar with the available tensions for dominants is crucial to understanding the sound of jazz harmony.

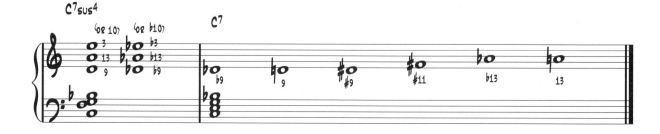

Tritone Substitutes and Other Common Chord Substitutions

Okay, almost done. All that remains is a few qualities of chord progressions. So far we've discussed half cadences and full cadences—and ii-7 V7 I. ii-7 V7's often occur in jazz. Sometimes they resolve to I and sometimes they move in different ways, such as up a half step or in minor thirds, but they are a sort of unit. When soloing over ii-7 to V7, jazz players often use Dorian for the minor ii chords and a darker scale for the V7. (Mixolydian on the V7 chord is the least spicy scale for dominants. It has the same notes as the Dorian over the ii chord). The most common substitute for a ii-7 to V to I Major 7th is the tritone substitute. "Tritone substitutes" mean replacing one or both chords in a ii-7 V7 with one or both chords of the ii-7 V7 located a tritone away. The reason that these chords are related is that they mirror each other. The Lydian b7 scale of a given dominant has the same notes as the altered scale of a dominant 7th that is a tritone away. So, if you are playing a Lydian b7 scale over a given dominant and then you play the altered scale over that same dominant, you are doing the same thing as playing a Lydian b7 over the first dominant and then playing the Lydian b7 scale over the dominant a tritone away. Anyway, all this is a way of saying that Db7 is like the altered version of a G7 chord. For this reason, D-7 to G7 can be changed to D-7 to Db7, or D-7 to Ab-7 to Db7 or any combination of progressions, as illustrated by the chart below.

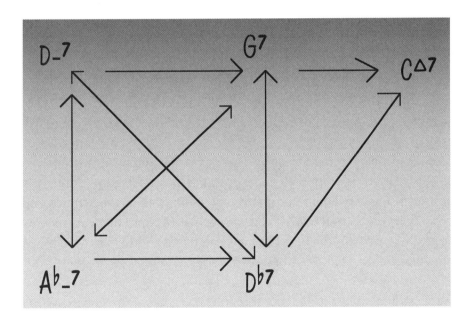

So tritone substitutes account for some of the chords you see in chord progressions that aren't chords we have discussed before, chords that aren't diatonic sevenths or secondary dominants. But we sometimes find some other chords in chord progressions—where do these come from? One whole class of chords are called modal interchange chords. These are chords that are diatonic to a scale other than the major scale, usually a parallel minor scale. We borrow these chords from the minor and bring them back to use in our major tonality. For example, the C natural minor scale gives us these diatonic sevenths: C-7, D-7b5, Eb major7, F-7, G-7, Ab Major7, Bb7.

Some of the most common modal interchange chords are:
1. iv-7 (and iv-6) which functions as a substitute for ii-7 (in C: F-7 (or F-6) leading to G7 to CMa7, where the F-6 is a replacement for a D-7 chord);
2. bVII7 which functions kind of similarly to the IV in plagal cadences, so it usually leads to I (as in the standard "Old Devil Moon" where (again in C) Cma7 to Bb7 is repeated several times at the beginning of the A section) and
3. #iv-7b5 (borrowed from the Lydian scale) is a kind of replacement for I (as in the common ending to a tune where the final I chord of the song is replaced by #iv-7b5 and then moves down chromatically to the end — D-7 G7 F#-7b5 FMa7 E-7 Eb7 D-7 G7 CMa7).

Diminished Sevenths

There's one other common chord that we need to talk about: the diminished 7th. Diminished chords function in several different ways. Sometimes diminished chords function as a substitute for a I chord that resolves to that I chord—they delay the resolution to the I chord. A more common use is as a passing diminished chord. For example, in the progression I Major7 to #i diminished to ii-7, the #i diminished 7th connects the two chords. It functions as a kind of V7 of ii-, something like a secondary dominant. In fact, you can substitute any V7 to I with a diminished 7th chord to I. The appropriate diminished 7th is found a half step below the target chord of the V7.

So, to recap: on a standard song we'd expect to find and be able to analyze diatonic triads and sevenths, secondary dominants and their related ii-7 chords, tritone substitutes, passing diminished chords and modal interchange chords, especially the iv-6, ii-7b5, #iv-7b5, and bVII7. If you can't explain a chord that you encounter as one of these things, perhaps the tune has modulated into another key (and the unexplained chord would then fit into one of these categories in the new key).

And that's it for our lightning tour through jazz theory! There are more things to talk about, like pentatonic scales, side slipping, bebop scales, non-available tensions (tensions that differ from the ones discussed above), Coltrane changes and slash chords. But, as an overall survey, we've probably covered 90 percent of the theory that jazz players commonly use. And we did it all in 5 pages, (Okay, 14, but who's counting?)

CHAPTER 2: *Problems in Jazz Practice*

Welcome to all of you who skipped the basic theory to get here. And to those of you that slogged through that chapter, hang in there, it's all downhill from here. (I'm never sure what that means...)

Problems are pretty easy to identify, and yet often students have no idea what to practice. As I said earlier, this book is about breaking down big difficult things into smaller, manageable, practicable things that you can master in a few minutes. There are two important skills here: 1) finding many different interesting and/or easy ways to approach a problem and 2) learning how to practice these various simpler approaches effectively.

Generating Lists of Things That Are Difficult

This is easy to do, very helpful, and yet most students never do it. If you are having trouble coming up with a list, you are probably not playing enough gigs. Going out on gigs, especially as a young musician, you are constantly confronted by things that you can't really do. For example, I remember the first time I played rhythm changes. I was in high school, living in Cleveland, and I got called to play at a vegetarian restaurant with an older bassist (a crazy bebopper type named Willis who had played with the great bebop pianist Barry Harris when he lived in New York) and a young alto player, so I dragged my Fender Rhodes piano down to the place to play for $25 and dinner. At some point, somebody called rhythm changes and I didn't know what that meant. The alto player opened a fake book to "Anthropology" and pointed and said, "there." When they counted the tune off, I was flabbergasted. How could anyone play over that many chords that fast? Needless to say, I probably didn't rock the joint on that particular tune.

(One more aside before we continue. I am always amazed at students who balk at playing gigs because they feel they aren't ready. My father, a lawyer and amateur pianist, perhaps hoping to discourage me from pursuing a career in music, but also from a sense of the moneymaking difficulties of the profession, drilled into me the notion that you don't ever say no to a gig if you aren't working. In addition to generating fuel for countless tales of my own misery and ineptitude, this work ethic helped me learn under fire, which is an invaluable experience).

Actually, a lot of what I know, I know because I had to work on it for a gig. "Giant Steps," playing in different keys, fast tempos, odd meter, intros—these are things that I only really started working on after an unsatisfactory experience on a gig somewhere.

I think some people have trouble with this concept. No one knows how to do everything. Of course, you need a certain amount of pluckiness when it comes to playing. A lot of guys who affect a pretty egotistical, "yeah, I am bad—what're YOU lookin' at?" attitude do very well. (As one successful bass player told me, people listen with their eyes). If you do have that kind of Alpha male attitude thing going on when you play, you'd be better off leaving it out of the practice room. Humility is the key there. You can only work on something once you admit that it needs work.

Of course, you don't have to be on a gig to identify productive things to work on. You can put on a CD and listen to your favorite players handle difficult rhythms, odd meters, harmonic complexity or anything else you can't yet do and get inspired to work on those things.

Not all of these things are problems per se. Some of these are simply things you are interested in. For example, it isn't really a problem if you don't use large intervals when you solo, but if you don't, that might be something that you want to incorporate into your practice. It might not be a problem if you don't use cross-rhythms or hemiolas, metric modulations and the like, but again, it might make your playing more interesting if you learn how to do these things. So what we are really talking about are things that you want to incorporate into your playing—things that have eluded you proceeding only by an intuitive approach. Some of these CAN be problems. Some of these things are just things that you might want to explore for yourself.

Returning to the question I posed earlier—the difficulty of practicing improvising— we can think about practicing improvising this way. The goal of practice should be to bring more playing elements into your comfort zone. You are tuning up and expanding the number of tools that are available to you while you are improvising.

The List

Here's a list of things that I think many students need to practice:

1 Chord change spelling
   a using scales, including bebop scales
   b using arpeggios
   c using chromatic approach notes
   d using guide-tone lines

2 Playing over complex chord progressions:
   a modulatory forms: tunes that go to several different keys
      (like "Body and Soul")
   b "Giant Steps" (changes that move very quickly)
   c forms with lots of alternate possibilities (such as rhythm changes or blues)

3 Playing fast tempos

4 Ear training

5 Creating more interesting left-hand comps (for pianists)
   a rhythmically
   b harmonically/melodically

6 Improving metronomic time and developing a deeper groove

7 Playing odd meters

8 Playing better in all keys

9 Developing a personal voice

10 Adding new material to your linear vocabulary
   a intervallically
   b rhythmically
   c harmonically

11 (for pianists) piano textures:
   a multi-line playing and inner lines in chordal passages
   b stride
   c bass lines

Of course, more things can be added to this list. If you are like me, new things that you want to work on will present themselves to you all the time. Also, a lot of these problems are interrelated. By that I mean, when I am working on rhythm changes I might be doing exercises that are aimed at developing my ears or playing with a deeper groove. Hopefully, everything I practice is leading me in the direction of developing a personal voice. So we'll attack some of the things on our list directly and some indirectly. But all this is just a lot of abstraction until we begin working on an actual problem, so let's begin.

CHAPTER 3: *The Importance of New Available Notes at the Point of Each Chord Change*

Let's take a simple but common form like the blues. If I want, I can start on the 9th of the I chord, on a C (in the key of Bb). I can hold this note through the whole blues form.

I've chosen one note that is consonant over the entire progression. I could have chosen others, such as F, Bb or G. Playing on the changes this way emphasizes the similar notes in each chord scale—the common tones. I often hear beginning jazz students soloing in this manner because restricting a solo to the notes that are common to a set of chords allows you to solo over the progression without changing scales. It makes soloing easier. When students construct solos over the blues that are entirely based on the blues scale they are exploiting this idea—using a single scale that works over every chord.

Common tone relationships are an important tool for soloing, one that we'll discuss more later, but on the most basic level, the sound of really nailing the chord changes is the sound of moving from an available note on one chord to a note that was previously unavailable but is now available on the next chord change. For example, if I play the 3rd on the first four bars of a basic blues form (in Bb a "D") and then flat that note in the 5th bar ("Db" on the Eb7—a b7), I am playing something that is a new available note—the Db which is consonant on the IV chord was dissonant on the I chord (albeit an acceptable blues scale note). The #11 on the IV chord ("A" on an Eb7) can be flatted to a b7 on the I chord in bar 7 (an "Ab" on the Bb7). The b7 on the five chord ("Eb" on the F7 chord) becomes a #11 or a 3 ("E"or"D") on the I chord. In all of these examples I am moving by half step to a note that wasn't available to me on the preceding chord change. Of course, I don't necessarily have to move by half step, but the important point is that I am moving (in this case by strong voice leading) from one available note to another emphasizing the new notes or the notes that are different.

Switching Chord Scales –
A New Set of Available Notes on Each New Chord

Knowing chord scales well is a little like being a harpist. (You get to wear a long white dress and lacy underthings...Hmm, maybe that's more information than you need to know about my practice routine). It's like being a harpist in that harpists must change their pedal settings for each new chord they encounter. Harps have 7 strings in each octave, so if a harp is going to solo through chord changes, the harpist must change his or her pedals for each chord change. This is an interesting way to look at soloing over chords—for each note: A B C D E F G, the note can be flat, sharp or natural. Which is it? Since the pedal setting effects every octave in the same way, once the pedals are set, you can hit any note on the instrument and be in the given scale. For example: A# B C# D# E F# G#, to A B C D E F# G to Ab Bb C D Eb F G would be the settings on the harp for the first two bars of "Giant Steps." This might explain why you don't hear a lot of harpists soloing over "Giant Steps," but it is a good metaphor for thinking about switching chord scales on a form with a lot of chords.

We want to develop the skill of recognizing quickly that a new set of notes is available for each new chord change. To do this, it helps to visualize the notes as a set of notes instead of a sequence of notes. In this way the piano differs from horns. On the piano, it is easier to think of a set of notes that exist at the same time. Horn players can conceive of a group of notes as easily as a pianist, but because they can only play one note at a time, they tend to think of chord scales as a group of consecutive notes one after the other moving upward or downward. What we really want to think of is the notes as a big bunch, like a cloud or a color out of a paintbrush. Of course, you can play them consecutively straight up the scale, but I find it more useful to visualize them as existing all over your instrument simultaneously, the way they do on a harp, and the way they do when you look at a C scale on the piano. Move your hand randomly around, striking only the white notes on the piano and you are playing notes from a C scale. (Put a brick on the sustain pedal and do it slowly and you may have a career in new age music.) When you know the chord scales well you can do this same thing with any scale, visualizing the groups of white and black notes that are available for you to play over each chord change.

I have heard this same idea attributed to George Benson, that when he thinks of a chord, the whole neck of his guitar lights up with the notes that are available to him—the chord scale of that particular chord. This is another good way to think of this process of familiarizing yourself with the available notes of scales.

Chord Scale Drills in Seven Steps

1. Working with the Bb blues above, play all the scales from the root of each chord out of time. How do we decide which scale to use on these changes? As stated above there are 5 common choices for dominant seventh scales: Mixolydian, Mixolydian #4 (also known as Lydian b7), b9 diminished (starting with the root and then a half step to the b9 and continuing by alternating whole and half steps), the 5th mode of the harmonic minor scale and the altered scale. You can experiment with these scales, trying different combinations on the chords of the blues, but here is a rough guide to go by. For the dominants that function as V7 to I or as a secondary dominant, use any of the above scales, but the more colorful scales will certainly work here (diminished or altered), and these scales lead more strongly to the next chord in the progression. For a dominant that is functioning as a I chord or as a IV chord use Mixolydian or mixo #4 as a first choice. For minor 7ths, Dorian is almost always a good choice.

So here are reasonable choices for the chord scales of the Bb blues: Bb7 (mixo), Eb7 (mixo), Bb7 (mixo), F-7 (Dorian), Bb7 (diminished), Eb7 (mixo), Bb7 (mixo), G7 (altered), C-7 (Dorian), F7 (diminished), Bb7 (mixo), G7 (altered), C-7 (Dorian), F7 (diminished).

2. Play each chord scale from the root in time, as 8th notes at a slow tempo (you only get 4 notes of the scale on the bars that have two chord changes in them).

3. Play each chord scale starting at a random place in the scale, but continuing straight up your instrument, meaning that if you start on the F on the first chord change (Bb7), then you'll play F G Ab Bb C D Eb F on the Bb7, then move to a G on the Eb7 and continue up the Eb7 scale. You'd be starting on an Ab in the 3rd bar (Bb7), and so on. You can switch direction whenever you start to get too high or low.

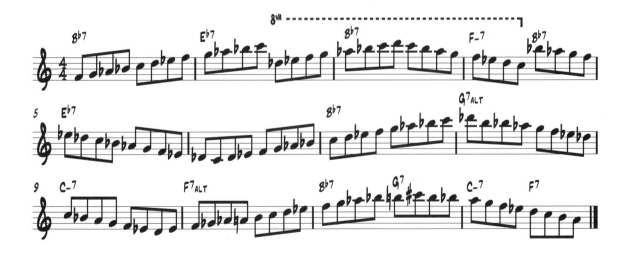

I call this the "big scale" exercise, for pretty obvious reasons (it's big and it's a scale). It's useful because it forces you to be specific about your scale choices and get out of the habit of visualizing scales as starting and ending in some particular place on your instrument.

4. You should also play the big scale exercise with different scales—use Lydian b7 instead of Mixolydian and altered instead of b9 diminished. Again, switch scale direction when you wish.

5. Play the big scale exercise using other rhythmic values such as triplets, half notes, and quarter notes. As you do this in time you'll be able to manage faster tempos.

It's interesting why having a lot of approaches to working on something helps. I think it has something to do with learning curves. When you don't know anything about something, getting to the point where you are marginally competent has a very shallow learning curve, meaning you get a lot of bang for your buck in your practicing, a lot of improvement for the amount of time you spend working.

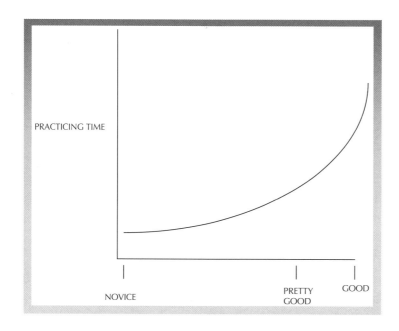

Practice tip #1

Have a lot of ways to practice each thing you are working on

This is an extremely important point, so I will make it about 50 more times in the course of this book. (But you still have to read about it now. Sorry). If you have more than one approach for working on a problem, you'll see improvement quicker. How do you start working on something that is new to you? One of Kenny Werner's mottos on this subject is very useful, "To get something you have to give up something." (Sadly, in life as well as in practicing. For example, last Christmas I shaved off my beard to make a wig to sell in order to have the money to buy a bottle of wine for my wife, but she sold her liver in order to buy me a beard trimmer). What Kenny means by this is that if I want to incorporate something new into my playing, I will have to give up some parameters of performance in order to work on this new problem. For example, if I am working on learning how to solo on "Giant Steps," I probably can't start out playing 8th note lines at a fast tempo. Maybe I can only play the melody. Maybe (if I am a pianist) I can only play the left hand. To make this point, I'll sometimes ask a beginning student to play "Giant Steps" and then count it off at a fairly quick tempo. Usually, the student caves in

As you get better, the amount of improvement relative to the amount of time you spend gets smaller. I think we've all experienced this—that starting out on something new has a big impact on your playing but over time the benefit from this particular approach lessens. Personally, I experienced this when I first began studying Japanese: the difference between knowing nothing and knowing a little was huge. As I moved toward the intermediate level, I would study a lot but feel relatively little change in my ability to communicate. So, when you bring a new approach to bear on a problem, you often get a little extra bonus of increased effectiveness.

The Little Scale

6. The next way to work on scales is with the "little scale." Maybe you can guess why I call it this. Okay, I'll tell you: because it's little and it's a scale. This is similar to the big scale idea, in that it focuses on changing scales quickly, on any part of your instrument. However, in this exercise we are more interested in voice leading from one scale to the next. The little scale is like looking at all of the scales through a hole in a fence. We are only interested in the part of the scale that falls in a hole the size of a 5th or 6th on the piano. So for example, let's take the 5th from middle C to the G above it. If I am playing a blues in Bb then the Bb7 scale has these notes: C D E F G (if it is a lydb7 scale and C D Eb F G if it is Mixolydian scale). The Eb7 scale would have C Db Eb F G and the Bb7 scale that leads to Eb7 in the 4th bar of the form would have Cb Db D E Gb (Bb7 altered). Bar 9 would be C D Eb F G and bar 10 (F13b9) could have C D Eb F F#). You get the idea. Play only the part of the scale that falls in the hole.

Tip #1 continued

and stops, saying he can't play it. But what is it that he can't play, or to put it another way, what CAN he play on "Giant Steps" at that tempo? Half notes? Maybe. In keeping with our motto, he has to sacrifice one of the parameters that is making it hard. He can probably play it slower. This is what students usually go to first and it IS very helpful to slow things down. But we can also give up other parameters aside from tempo. We could play less of the form, maybe only the first two bars and loop them at a fast tempo, or we could play fewer notes, again without sacrificing tempo (half notes, quarters, adding rests, etc.). Each of these methods will address the problem in a different way than by slowing it down. Having more than one method for cutting a difficult problem down to size is one of the key skills of becoming a better practicer.

Practice tip #2
Effortlessness

Practice works best when you are practicing at a level where whatever you are working on is EASY. If it still feels difficult then you probably haven't simplified the problem enough. You can only internalize musical changes when what you are working on is as close to effortless as possible. Most students haven't experimented enough with finding the level where playing is truly effortless. I mentioned Kenny Werner a few paragraphs ago, and he has made a big impact on a lot of students studying jazz by promoting the importance of developing the quality of effortlessness in playing. I first met Kenny when I was in High School. Nine or ten years later when I moved to New York, I studied with him for a couple of years. Lessons with Kenny focused on touching the piano without effort. Instead of working on complex technical issues, we started with a simple Hanon (C, D, E, F, G, F, E, D, C) trying to find a way to play this without any (or with minimal) effort. Ultimately, exploring playing with the least possible effort opened up a lot of things in my playing. To paraphrase the Effortless Master himself, good practicing means that you are always practicing effortlessness

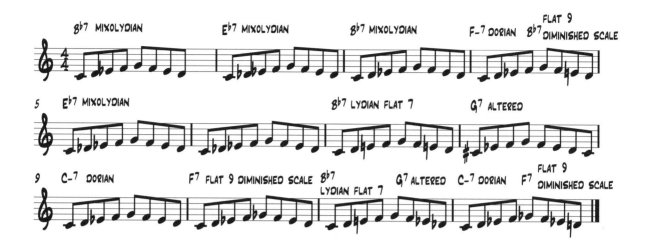

(Of course, you don't have to play these scale fragments going up and down as written above. You can play the little scale notes as clusters simultaneously, or vary the order of notes to make lines that interest you).

The little scale exercise helps us view what happens to a piece of your instrument's range as it morphs from one chord to another. If I take several different holes of different sizes, I will cover all the parts of each scale.

Tip #2 continued

through the medium of whatever you happen to be working on. So if you are practicing scales, think that you are practicing being effortless at the piano through the medium of practicing scales. It was fascinating to see the way Kenny's ideas have been embraced by students since the publication of his book and his emergence as a teacher on an international scale. I think it speaks to the need for attention on the meditative and psychological aspects of playing, and I would encourage students interested in pursuing this line further to pick up Kenny Werner's "Effortless Mastery."

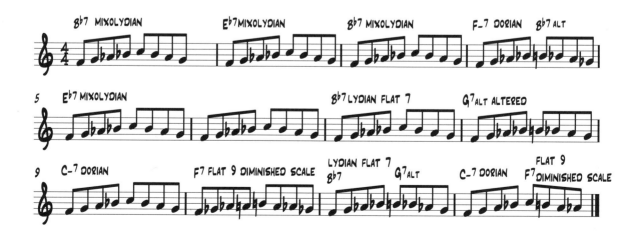

Working with the little scale is like taking one note, "A" for example, and seeing what happens to it on each chord. A is flat for the Bb7 change, natural for the Eb7#11(if you happen to be thinking Lydian flat 7 scale here—with the option of being flat if we want a Mixolydian sound). It's flat again for the F-7 to Bb7 ii-7 V7 in bar 4 and then again (optionally) natural for the Eb7. If we have an Ediminished 7 in bar 6, then it is natural, and then flat again for the Bb7 in bar 7. For the G7 in bar 8, A is flat if the scale is altered. For the 9th bar, C-7, A is natural, and then in bar 10, it is either flat or natural (Ab is #9 on the F7 altered and A natural is 3 on the F7 altered). For the turnaround at the end, the A is flat for the first two chords, natural for the 3rd chord and either natural or flat for the last chord in the turnaround. And that is the story of A over the Bb blues form.

Practice tip #3

The functions of a note relative to a certain bass note.

I once saw a Star Trek episode where there was a woman who seemed to be able to see but was in fact blind. (This came in handy for her because she was traveling with a really ugly guy that she could look at that no one else could look at without going crazy and

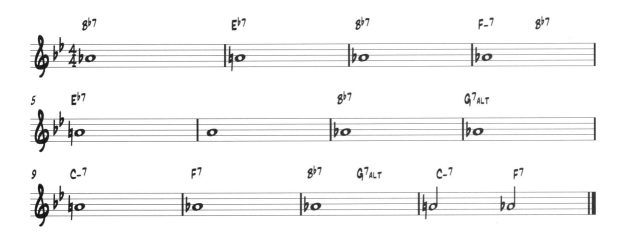

If you followed the story of all the other notes through the blues form you'd have some useful information for building a solo over this form. (Try this on your own, taking each note and seeing where it is natural and where it is sharped or flatted). Please keep in mind that in all the above examples, I am making choices about using particular chord scales. There is no right and wrong here, although I am using the guidelines that we discussed on page 27, that if a dominant doesn't resolve down a fifth to the next chord, it gets Mixolydian or Lydian b7 (more likely to be Lydian b7 if it isn't the I chord), and if the dominant chord does resolve down a fifth, then it will be more likely that it gets the altered scale or the half/whole diminished scale. Still, you should try all of the chord scales that are available to you and let your ear choose which ones have the sound that you want to use.

Spock looked at him and seemed to go crazy but didn't because Vulcans have an extra set of eyelids that are vestigial—but I digress, although I am thrilled to have been able to use the word "vestigial" in this book). Anyway, she managed to fool everyone into thinking that she could see because she had a sensor grid dress that allowed her to know where everything was in relation to her. So, if she was standing by the communications console on the bridge, say, she could tell from her sensors that the elevator was exactly 3 feet and 4 inches to her right, and the console that controlled the photon torpedoes was exactly 5 feet and

7. Complete the big scale and small scale exercises by using all sorts of rhythmic values—8th notes, quarter notes, half notes, triplets—and by using all of the different scale possibilities you can think of. By now, you should be well on your way to having a good grasp of the available chord scales for this form in this key. You too, like George Benson, should be able to look at your instrument, follow the form of the blues and have the appropriate keys light up mentally. Ultimately, this sort of familiarity with scales will help you to be able to forget about theory when you play.

SCALE PRACTICE WRAP UP

1 Play scales out of time (ascending and descending) for each chord.
2 Play scales in time in 8th notes (start at a slow tempo).
3 Play the scales starting anywhere, continuing straight up your instrument (the big scale exercise).
4 Play the big scale exercise using different scales for each chord.
5 Play the big scale exercise in different rhythmic values (triplets, 16th notes, etc.).
6 Play all of the scales within the range of a fifth or sixth (the small scale exercise).
7 Play the small scale exercise varying scale options, rhythmic values and note order.

Bebop Scales

The next step is to add some notes that aren't in the scales. Very often, jazz musicians are subdividing at the level of 8th notes, meaning, their lines are filled with 8th notes. (The relationship of 8th notes (soloist) to quarter notes (walking bass notes) is one of the most fundamental relationships in defining swing rhythm). Most scales, on the other hand have 7 notes. So if you play a 7 note scale starting on the root in 8th notes for two bars the downbeats of the measure fall like this:

Because every note in the scale gets emphasized the same amount over the two bar period, playing up and down the scale tends to sound a little aimless.

Tip #3 continued

9 inches to her left. If she moved, her position relative to those two things would change and the new values would be say, 6 feet and 8 inches for the elevator and 9 feet 2 and 1/2 inches for the console (although this being set in the future you'd imagine that everything would finally be metric). What does this have to do with chords? Well, jazz students need to develop this type of grid to find all of the tensions and scale tones relative to a particular bass note. If I input a bass note, say G, then I need to know instantly that Eb is the b6 (or b13), B is the 3rd and F# is the major 7th. If I change the bass note, all of these relationships immediately change so if the bass note changes to an Eb, say, now Eb is a 1, B is a b6 (or b13) and F# (Gb) is a minor 3rd (or #9). You can practice this easily at a piano. (This is easy even for non-pianists.) Play any bass note with your left hand and drop your right hand somewhere on the right side of the keyboard. Practice naming the right hand pitch in relation to the bass note you are playing. This will help develop your theoretical sense of this grid or series of interval relationships. Another way to work on this is to play a random bass note and imagine a particular note—the #11 or the 9th, say. Keep thinking of different pitches and checking them to see if you were able to hear them correctly. Developing this sort of rapidly changing grid (in both the theoretical and aural senses) in all keys helps make playing over changes possible. And without it, looking at a complex (or "ugly" tune harmonically, to strain the Star Trek metaphor to the breaking point), you will go crazy like Spock unless you have a vestigial set of eyelids.

If we add a half step to the scale we get a different pattern:

In this last example, the chord tones of the I Maj6th chord are emphasized so the line sounds less aimless and more directional. The strong beats define the chord sound.

These kinds of scales with one added chromatic approach note are called bebop scales. The common notes to add to make bebop scales are #5 in the case of scales that have a major 7th in them (major and melodic minor) and the major 7 in scales that have a flatted 7th (Mixolydian, Dorian, Lydian b7, altered).

Practice tip #4
Only practice when you are interested in what you are working on

Monitoring your level of engagement with what you are working on is another important skill that good practicers possess. It has to be fun. Really, it HAS to be FUN. Keep in mind that you can keep switching approaches to the problem. Try to find ones that are fun for you. If you are bored you won't retain much information, not to mention you are passing your life in misery. (This is somewhat unavoidable; see: the Buddha, life is misery section). This is the mindset to which Kenny Werner's Effortless Mastery approach has been such a good antidote. A long time ago, one of my first teachers told me that practicing had to be fun to be effective and I didn't believe him, just as I imagine a lot of you don't believe me now when I say that it is possible to practice everything that you want to work on and have fun at the same time. And the things that aren't fun to work on? Don't practice them. There is enough to do working on things that are interesting and enjoyable. Still, try to stay open to what might make the thing that isn't fun fun. There are a lot of reasons why some things don't seem like much fun to work on, but probably the main thing that keeps them from being fun is that they are too difficult. Things that are too difficult are things that you haven't figured out how to break down into smaller simpler problems. If you are breaking down big problems into easy to solve small ones that you can whip through in a few minutes, you are probably having fun, because you are having success. Failure, on the other hand, is rarely fun, so if you are miserable that might be a good indication that things are not working out so well for you in the practice department.

For example, in the above steps for improving familiarity with scales, the desire to get through all of the steps might make you impatient. You might skip the first two steps.

Sometimes the major 3rd is added to the Dorian minor scale instead of the 7th.

So now you should practice all of the above scale exercises with bebop scales: big scale, small scale, everything you know. We are going to want to have these steps clearly in mind when we start working on practicing a new new chord progression so let's review these now. **(CD EXAMPLE 1: Bebop scales over Bb blues)**

Whenever you are practicing rudiments such as this, try to practice them as long as it seems interesting and useful to you.

Bebop-like Scales

The next approach to scale practice involves taking the idea of bebop scales and applying it in a freer way. Adding a chromatic note tends to make the next note (the one the chromatic note is leading to) more important, and so bebop scales have more of a sense of direction than diatonic scales. (They create a hierarchy of values to the notes you are playing, so that some notes sound like leading tones and other notes sound like the target of the previous note). I can add chromatic pitches other than those prescribed by the bebop scales and improvise combinations of scale and chromatic passing tones that have enough scale passages to retain the sound of the scale and have enough chromaticism to give those scale lines more of a sense of direction. When you listen to great jazz players from the 1950s to the present, you hear this use of chromaticism as a way of creating direction in scalar passages. **(CD EXAMPLE 2: Bebop-like scales over Bb blues)**

Tip #4 continued

Working on the big scale exercise, you might hurry through, not specifically delineating which scale you are using on each chord. As I listen to a student going through the motions of practicing in this fashion, I'll often suggest that he or she do less. We might work only on 2 bars, the G7 altered going to the C-7, for example. Can you connect these two chords with eighth notes in a smooth, easy way? How can varying the direction of the line make it sound more interesting? Working within these relatively confining parameters, what's the best line you can improvise? Now, using the small scale for the same two bars, let's try different ranges to see where interesting points of intersection between these two scales lie. You can pick any 5th-sized portion of the scale and some places will contain more common tones between the two scales, and other places will have more changing tones. Which one interests you?

As we slow things down and explore small pieces of the harmony, practicing becomes more interesting, creative and fun. I am probably one of the least detail-oriented people that I know (you should see how messy my car is), but in practicing, a lot of the fun comes from working with small details—like tiny changes in intervals and rhythms. Developing an interest in these details leads you to a deeper understanding of music fundamentals and makes you a better improviser.

I think this step is extremely important for students to grapple with. In general, the use of chromatic pitches eludes a lot of younger players, giving their lines a "floating in the scale," somewhat bland, diatonic quality.

To make this step clearer, let's look at an example. Here is a scalar solo that incorporates chromatic approach notes in the freer bebop-scale-like way that I am suggesting. Notice that sometimes I used the chromatic approach notes found in bebop scales (bar 5, bar 10, bar 12), but many more chromatic approach notes are added.

If you add too many chromatic approach notes it will sound like you are playing a chromatic scale over all of the harmony and aren't really defining the chord scale sounds. Being able to add chromatic approach notes whenever you want while maintaining the sound of the chord scale means finding a balance point between the chromatic scale and the chord scale.

If you've tried all of the above approaches to working on scales, you should have made some progress at spelling chords more effectively. Pianists have the ability to define harmony with their left hands, but should also be able to play lines that go through the heart of each chord without relying on the left hand to define the harmony. With the right hand alone, pianists should be able to define the chord progression harmonically (and melodically) as exactly and beautifully as a horn player, clearly outlining the harmony of a song. The scalar things that we have been working on should help all instrumentalists be able to do this.

Arpeggios

By "arpeggio" I really mean interval skips that are larger than a whole step. Taken together with scales and chromatic approach notes, these three categories make up all of the possible material of a solo. Sometimes it is useful to analyze a student's solo on the basis of what elements are the most present in the mix. Does the player rely more on chromaticism, scale or arpeggiation? How about some of your favorite soloists, which are most prevalent in their solos: scales, skips or half steps?

By asking yourself which of these things contribute the most to your soloing you can find new directions to emphasize in your practice. If, for example, you feel you tend to play more arpeggios than scales in your solos, you should focus on the scale work we've been discussing. At the same time, you can try to extend what you have been doing with arpeggios to another level of complexity by following some of the suggestions below.

Arpeggio Practice in 6 Steps

There are really 4 different types of arpeggios to practice: 1) diatonic triads or diatonic 7ths and their inversions; 2) the big chord that can be built out of every scale when arranged in 3rds (1,3,5,7,9,11,13) and different pieces of that chord (including inversions); 3) upper structure triads and 4) arpeggios based on 4ths or other intervals larger than a third.

1. Diatonic triad and seventh practice. As we went over in the theory section, diatonic triads are the triads that occur when you build a root third and fifth on each step of the scale. So, for the first triad you'd play 135; for the second you'd play 246, then 357, 461(8), 572(9), 61(8) 3(10) and 72(9) 4(11).

For diatonic 7ths you use the same principle, but instead of finding the triad that is built on each step, you are finding the seventh chord: 1357, 2461(8), etc.

Diatonic 7ths and triads are used a lot in soloing. As you remember from the discussion of bebop scales, the number of notes in the scale is sometimes very important for how the scale gets used in a bar of 4/4. For this reason, the four-note 7th arpeggios are frequently played as 8th notes. The steps to mastering these arpeggios are very similar to the first steps in working on scales. First play them all for each scale starting on the root and out of time. Second, play them as 8th notes at a slow tempo and start with the seventh chord that is built on the root of the scale. For the second chord, try continuing with the seventh chord that is built on the next scale note up or down from the previous chord. For example, for our blues in Bb, the first bar would be an arpeggiation of Bb7 to C-7. The second bar (Eb7) would be Dbmaj7#5 (if you are using the chord scale Lydian b7) to Eb7. The third bar would be F-7 (or F-Maj7 if you are using a Bb Lydian b7 scale) to G-7. The 4th bar: Abmaj7 to Bb7; 5th bar (changing direction here and whenever you wish): C-7 to Bb-7(or Bb-maj7 if you are playing an Eb7 or Adiminished 7th to Gdiminished 7th if you are playing an Ediminished chord in this bar). Et cetera. Here it is written out, continuing on through the rest of the chorus:

Practice tip #6

The inverted Y: the "forking paths" concept, or a dialectical approach to practice

Very often in practice, we encounter a tendency, something that we like or something that we do that

Being able to switch diatonic sevenths at any particular place you happen to be in the chord scale is a variation of the scalar exercise of being able to switch chord scales at any place you happen to be.

Another way to work with this concept is to vary the order of the notes in the diatonic seventh. Instead of always ascending in the 1,3, 5, 7 order, we could move the notes around: 1,5,3, 7 or 7, 3, 1, 5. Exploring different permutations of the 7th chords changes the quality of the line, as seen in the example below.

is unconscious, but in either case is an identifying feature of our playing. In this regard I am reminded of a student who came to me to work on composition. He brought in a Latin tune he had written. It had an intro with an ostinato bass line under a dominant sus4 chord that repeated for 4 bars and then went up a whole step for another 4 bars. The harmony of the rest of the tune was a sort of modified "Autumn Leaves" progression—ii-V I major, ii-V-i minor. The

Another way to create melodic variations is to change the rhythms of the above 8th note patterns.

2. The arpeggio built in thirds, chord tones plus extensions. This is just to say that any chord can be stacked in thirds, 1,3,5,7,9,11,13.

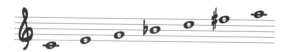

Actually this large chord is really the same as the first two diatonic 7ths of a scale—the diatonic sevenths built on the first and second degrees of the scale—but it is also useful to think of it as one big chord, the arpeggio of all the notes available to you in a scale. Since we are dealing with stacked thirds that are diatonic, there really isn't anything new here, nothing that we haven't encountered in the last step. It's just a different way of thinking about the same theoretical information. For every chord change, you can imagine this big chord comprised of all the chord tones and tensions, and start your arpeggio anywhere you want. If you are thinking in 4-note groupings, you can play from the 3rd to the 9th, from the 5th to the 11th, from the 7th to the 13th or any other grouping of 4 notes from the big arpeggio of all the available notes. These pieces of the big arpeggio on each chord are useful when you are practicing in a pattern oriented way. Also each of these chords have their own sound—the quality they possess as a kind of 7th chord plus their relationship to the root of the chord.

Tip #6 continued

melody featured a lot of upbeats. The next week, he wrote another Latin tune. This one had an intro that had an ostinato bass line and went to 2 keys, I think up a half step. The melody was a sort of ii-V-I major and relative minor progression a lot like the week before. I asked him to write another tune and described the exact plan that he had used (two times with slight variations) above. "Hmmmm," he said; he would try. I then pointed out that he had already written two songs using this exact same structure without being aware of it. "Huh," he said.

We all have such tendencies, even if we aren't all so eloquent about them. Usually when we discover a tendency of that sort we try to do the opposite, to squelch the previously unnoticed but, now that we are aware of it, offensive quality. This, I think, is a mistake. Tendencies are useful. They reveal an interest, a potential direction. Also, our desire to root out these tendencies makes us reluctant to go looking for them, and becoming aware of these tendencies helps us to find ones that have become habitual and limiting. I find that it's usually more helpful to notice the tendency and then go in two different directions. One direction is to embrace the tendency. Let's say that at a certain tempo I tend to play a lot of triplets. I notice that some other musicians whose

For example, on a dominant 7 #11 chord, the arpeggio that starts on the 7th is a Major7#5,

the arpeggio that starts on the 5th is a minorMajor7

and the arpeggio that starts on the 3rd (and the one that starts on the #11 as well) is a min7 b5 chord.

Finding the parts of the scale that have a distinctive or unusual chord quality allows you to bring out different colors that are buried inside the chord scale. So try soloing with all minor7b5 chords, moving from one part of the large arpeggio for each chord to another, or try to find Major7#5 sounds over each chord. Having a particular upper structure seventh chord quality in mind can also have an impact on which chord scale you choose; for example, if you want to make Major7#5 upper structures over dominant seventh chords, it's easier if you use the altered scale or Lydian b7 scale.

3. I want to also underline two things here as we look at these diatonic 7ths and the big chord available with all the scale notes stacked in thirds. One is that triads can be built starting on any of the scale degrees or parts of the big chord. Try playing all of the diatonic triads in 2 octaves. It's important to have access to these triads as well as 7th chords and tensions. After a particularly chromatic passage, or if the harmony starts to feel obscure, or if you are playing "outside" the chord changes (more on that later), you might want to return to the harmony in a strong, simple and clear way, and triads are a means of doing that. Of course, triads are beautiful structures in themselves—not all interesting or beautiful lines are harmonically complex or have a lot of tensions in them.

rhythmic approach I admire are playing things other than triplets at the same tempo. Instead of abandoning triplets, I'll work on different aspects of playing triplets. I'll bring in accents, or add rests in unusual places, or try metric modulation by triplet, perhaps work on going from quarter note triplets to 8th note triplets. At the same session, though, I'll try to experiment with some rhythms that I tend not to play. I'll try quarters and halves. I'll practice playing all non-triplet time values. Do these rhythms feel less comfortable for me? Very often when I start working on something that is different from my habitual tendency it does feel a bit uncomfortable. How can I bring these new things (in this case, rhythmic values at a particular tempo) into my comfort zone? We'll go into more of this when we discuss rhythmic approaches to practice, but for now, let me just say that this is a model for practicing that I use constantly. Find something. Define it. Practice that thing. Practice its opposite. I think of it as a forking path, or as an inverted "Y." The thing that you are interested in leads to more of itself—or a more fully investigated version of

itself—and to its opposite, or more accurately, since a lot of these things don't exactly have opposites, to something different from the thing in question. So in the case of the student composer above, I'd say try to write the ultimate tune using the game plan that you've been employing unconsciously. Then try to define the opposite way. In this case, writing a tune with no intro, or perhaps a harmonic progression that doesn't suggest any tonic. How about a series of chord changes that never employ V to I? Anyway, once you start trying to define what is the opposite path—the ways you haven't been using—you are off to the races and

4. It's important to look at all of these triads and sevenths in different inversions as well. When we invert triads, we are essentially shuffling a 4th around a couple of 3rds. (In a major triad, for example, the root position triad has a major 3rd on the bottom, a minor 3rd after that and a 4th up to the root. In the second inversion we have a minor 3rd on the bottom and then a 4th and then a major third up to the root. In the second inversion we have a 4th on the bottom and then a major 3rd and a minor 3rd up to the root.)

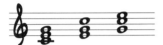

When we invert 7ths we end up with combinations of 3rds and 2nds instead of all stacked thirds.

So, practice the things you've worked on with diatonic 7ths using all of the inversion options open to you.

5. Another interesting arpeggio option is found in upper structure triads. An upper structure triad is a triad, usually major, that works over a 7th chord. These are also sometimes written as slash chords. Essentially your options are C/C, Db/C, D/C, Eb/C, E/C, F/C, Gb/C, G/C, Ab/C, A/C, Bb/C and B/C. (Some of these chords don't tell us much that is new: C/C is simply C and F/C is an F triad in 2nd inversion).

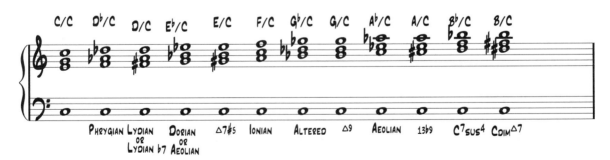

Each of these chords implies a certain harmony as shown in the example above. Arrangements of triads over bass notes are striking both when used melodically or when played in a piano voicing because we hear some of the bitonality of their structure. When you play A /C (put the A triad in second

Tip #6 continued
the ideas come flooding in.

In a similar situation with a student who had a strong left hand but a weaker right hand line concept, we did a whole series of left hand things from 8th notes against a right hand melody to walking bass at various tempos. At the same time we worked on right hand soloing alone or over whole note roots in the left hand. When we first started working together, the student had been trying only to work on right hand oriented things, because he felt like his left hand was pretty strong. When we started doing both, it put his playing in perspective. After all, his left hand wasn't like Art Tatum's or anything, so developing the left hand further made sense—he could still improve and he was more likely to spend profitable time on that because he was confident that he would be successful with it. So, in short, practice both what you are good at and what you are not good at.

We will use this method many more times in the course of this book. Perhaps now is a good time for you to analyze some of your own strengths as a jazz player. For example, maybe you are pretty conversant in playing over ii-V-I type progressions such as "Bye Bye Blackbird" or "Secret Love." A way to develop this strength fur-

ther might be to move some of these comfortable progressions into keys that you are less comfortable with. Another way might be to focus on some tunes that have very fast moving ii-V-I progressions, like "Mo-

inversion so that we hear the E as a third of the C root), you hear the two tonalities ringing against each other and it makes a brilliant sound.

6. Of course, arpeggios can be made of intervals other than 3rds. Arpeggios that are based on 4ths can be used to create interesting diatonic lines. (Just as in the case of diatonic thirds that included both major and minor 3rds, if you start building scales out of 4ths, you'll need to use tritones in some situations to conform to the chord scale.) Here are diatonic 4ths for 4 different C scales. The asterisks (*) are placed above the diatonic 4ths that are composed entirely of perfect 4ths. It is interesting to know which scale degrees generate diatonic 4ths that have no tritones in them. Try constructing a line from these diatonic 4ths and then add diatonic fourth chords that have tritones in them. See what you like, which sounds are interesting to you.

(CD EXAMPLE 3: Diatonic 4ths over Bb Blues)

Tip #6 continued

ment's Notice" or "Lazybird." Can you play equally well over ii-V-I progressions where the chords come two to a bar, or one chord to a bar? A way to work on the opposite of this strength might involve working on a particular scale, perhaps an unusual scale that you don't play as often, over a pedal or modal situation. Another opposite idea might be to focus on improvising with certain intervals over a pedal or in a free harmonic situation. We will discuss these different ways to practice later in the course of the book, but for now I suggest that you begin thinking yourself of ways to both extend what you do already in interesting directions and to imagine the opposites of these things—things that you don't yet do but are interested in trying.

Of course, diatonic 5ths, 6ths and combinations of intervals can be selected to break up the scale into interesting skips and leaps. Sometimes it is interesting to pick a few intervals, like 4ths, 5ths and 2nds, and see how far you can go working your way through a chord progression focusing on these sounds. Thinking intervallically is a rich source of material for solos, and you should spend a lot of time playing with this, seeing what sounds are most compelling for you.

Practice tip #7
Rhythmic interlude

Just like developing your ear, developing greater rhythmic awareness can be incorporated into whatever you are working on. In the above discussion of diatonic seventh chords (starting on page 36), the 4 note seventh chords sit very squarely in 4/4 meter. They also very clearly define the harmony, since when you play two adjacent diatonic seventh chords you have played all of the notes of the scale. Try displacing the above seventh chords one 8th note, so that the first diatonic 7th in the bar begins on the "and" of one. This throws all of the other seventh chords off one 8th note as shown in the example here:

For pianists, play the root on one in the left hand so that you don't lose your place in the form. Try other displacements—try starting one 8th note early on the "and" of 4 or try displacements of a quarter note in either direction. Try playing these 4-note groupings as triplets. These kind of devices are called cross rhythms or hemiolas. (More on that later in the rhythm section). (For a very famous example of 4-note arpeggiations in triplets see Herbie Hancock's "All of You" solo on Miles Davis Live at Carnegie Hall.) One of the values of working on cross rhythms or other types of rhythmic complexity is that they make you feel more comfortable in 4/4 situations. They seat you more definitively in the 4/4 (or in any meter that you are working on for that matter). **(CD EXAMPLE 4: 8th note displacements of diatonic 7th arpeggiations over Bb Blues)**

ARPEGGIO PRACTICE WRAP UP

So let's quickly review the suggestions for practicing arpeggios.

1 Diatonic 7ths
   a Practice in 8th notes over the chord progression of the blues, starting on the first degree of the scale and moving up.
   b Start on any degree of the scale.
   c Displace an 8th note rhythmically (meaning, start on the "and" of one or the "and" of four).
   d Practice steps a, b and c in each inversion.
   e Compose a solo using diatonic sevenths as the primary ingredient.

2 The big chord (chord tones and scale tones together)
   a Practice playing the whole arpeggio for each chord change.
   b Try singing the arpeggio.
   c Break the arpeggio into four note units (1 3 5 7, 3 5 7 9, 5 7 9 11, 7 9 11 13). and practice each unit over all of the chords of the progression.
   d Practice steps a, b and c in each inversion.

3 Upper structure triads
   a Practice arpeggiating upper structure triads wherever the progression allows.
   b Practice above step in all inversions.

4 Diatonic 4ths
   a Practice as diatonic 7ths above (only perfect 4ths).
   b Practice as diatonic 7ths above (perfect 4ths and combinations of 4ths and tritones.
   c Practice all inversions of b.

Finally, though, these are just suggestions for incorporating arpeggiation into your practicing. Using different inversions, stacking different intervals and other rhythmic displacements, you can generate lines that come from your own musical taste. Before you leave this topic, spend some time exploring possibilities that we haven't examined in this section.

Chromatic Approach Notes

We have already encountered chromatic approach notes when we were discussing bebop scales. Taken together with arpeggios and scales, they round out pretty much everything that it is possible to play in a solo (at least everything that can be analyzed harmonically).

Chromatic approach notes were an important bebop innovation. They inject a strong element of chromaticism into change playing. That's one of the things that made bebop so foreign to older musicians of the time. Chromatic approach notes give us a way to bring all 12 pitches to any tonal situation. By using chromatic approach notes, you can play a C natural on a Bmajor 7th chord as well as other notes that take you outside of the chord scale, while still playing "inside" the chord changes. Chromatic approach notes are short visits to sounds outside of the chord scale, that resolve back to notes in the given chord scale.

My first sense of the importance of these notes to the bebop vocabulary came when I was in junior high school. I was torn between playing folk guitar and jazz piano. I was more developed as a pianist (I didn't even read music on guitar and couldn't tell you the notes of the fingerboard without doing considerable thinking about it—I read tablature), but socially and politically I liked where folk music was coming from. (I was listening to people like Stefan Grossman, Rev. Gary Davis and Pete Seeger). So I played guitar for a few years, but as I became more serious about piano and jazz, my guitar playing atrophied. Occasionally, I would pick up the guitar and try to play something jazz-like on it. When I tried to solo over changes, my lack of familiarity with the fingerboard would mess me up, and so I was always missing the note I wanted by a half step or a whole step and correcting it by ear. Listening to these lines with their mistakes and fixes, I noticed that they sounded a lot more bebop-like than my piano soloing, which was pretty diatonic at the time. Aha! This was interesting. For me, studying jazz has been filled with these sorts of discoveries, and the first time I came across chromatic approach notes was one such epiphany. (There were a lot of other epiphanies along the way, like the first time I figured out that a 13 b9 voicing—E/G7—was a sound I knew from an Oscar Peterson record, the first time someone showed me a 4th voicing or left hand 3-note voicings, the first time

Practice tip #8
More tools

For anything that you are working on, you always have several different tools to explore it. To bring a more ear-oriented approach to the problem, try singing. For non-horn players, sing the 7th chord as you play it, note by note up the arpeggio. (Horn players: imagine each note before you play it.) Play the chord and then listen internally as you sing it silently in your head. Or just look at your instrument and imagine the sound clearly and then play it and see if you were correct. If when you play the sound it differs from what you imagined it would sound like, figure out what it was that you heard and analyze it. Maybe you missed an interval of a 4th and sang the 5th instead. Note the mistake and practice the same intervals over each chord change. This is important. One of the problems with working on ear training is that it is often presented as a kind of a test. What is this chord? Right! What is this interval? Wrong! Repeat. Testing yourself over and over in this fashion doesn't really constitute practicing. It is practicing of a sort, but it is not a very clear or organized way to develop your ears. Integrating ear training into your practice offers another way to work on your ears—a way that allows you to find another avenue for practicing this "hard-to-practice" thing. One of the most common melodic ear training mistakes comes from confusion about whether the sound that you are hearing is over one chord in a progression or the key that you are playing in. If you are playing a blues and you are on the 5th bar and you hear a minor 3rd in the line that you want to play, is it the minor 3rd of the key or the minor 3rd of the IV chord? As the chords become more complex, these mistakes become more common. So let's say you are imagining the notes of a chord and you make a mistake, meaning that the sound that you imagined isn't what you hear when you play the arpeggio. What was the note that you heard? Let's say you were hearing these pitches in an arpeggio: the 9th, the b7th and 13th. When

I learned what a diminished scale was. I guess these things were epiphanies because I had been listening to a lot of jazz but didn't really understand it. When someone showed me something, or when I figured out something that I had heard, a lot of times it hit me with a revelatory force. Aha! So that's what that sound is. In these days of jazz education where students read jazz books and get a lot of resources handed to them, I wonder if these epiphanies still occur).

Anyway, to get back to my second chromatic-approach-related epiphany, I went to Berklee music school for a couple of semesters, and the first assignment my piano teacher gave me was to transcribe a Bud Powell solo by ear in the library (away from the piano), sitting at an old Wollensack reel-to-reel tape recorder. It had half speed, which helped a lot, but as I listened to the solo I had the sense that Bud was playing notes that weren't on the piano—that he had found notes that were in the cracks. I had heard this music before then, of course, but somehow I hadn't quite figured out what was essential to the sound I was hearing. Once again, it was the chromaticism that I hadn't really "heard" before.

To repeat something that we talked about earlier in relation to bebop scales, chromatic approach notes give directionality to a solo. They also are essential rhythmically, creating accent patterns by putting important target notes on the downbeat (or upbeats if you so choose) of a measure. Perhaps on an even more basic level, they create a hierarchy of note values—by which I mean, they create a sense of certain notes in the line being more important than others—some notes becoming the target or destination of the line. They also give the soloist a lot of material because, combined with scales or arpeggios, they generate countless variations and lines over a given chord.

Let's take a line by Bud Powell from the same solo that I had to transcribe in the library that I spoke about earlier:

Tip #8 continued

you went to play this fragment, you played something else. Okay, now play the root to each chord change and imagine the 9th, b7th and 13th of the new chord. Change the 9th, 7th and 13th to fit the chord scale you are using for each chord, so maybe you missed a natural 9th, b7th and natural 13th on the IV7 chord but in bar 8 you are trying to hear the b9, b7th and b13th over the VI7(altered) chord. Once you have gone through these problematic notes with each chord, your ears will feel sharper, and you've escaped from the ear training test mode and have actually practiced working on these problematic sounds for you on different chords.

Practice tip #9
Meet the composer

Another tool is composition. After working on the scale exercise or the displaced diatonic 7th chords above, you could compose a chorus where you try to create the most interesting combination of chord scale and chromatic note choices, or the most interesting displacements. Composing helps you glimpse your soloing years in the future when you have a better handle on the things that you are working on now (when food will come in little pill forms and we'll all be driving hover crafts to the gig). Unfortunately, when you play at a gig that includes dinner, the little food pills they serve the band will not be the same little food pills that are on the regular menu. (But I digress.) In that way, it helps you to solidify your sense of what you like and what direction you want to go in. Use any of the exercises in this book, or better yet, ideas of your own, as a jumping off place for a composition. (For an example of this, see the chorus of blues solo that utilizes 8th note displacements as an organizing feature on the top of page 38.)

This line shows a skillful blending of chromatic approach notes, scales and arpeggios. As illustrated below, it starts with a Bb pentatonic scale with one note added above and below the first target note. This pattern delays the arrival of the 3rd until beat 3 in the measure. Then we get an unusual arpeggiation from the 3rd to the #11 (a piece of our big arpeggio), a scale fragment (which could also be considered a chromatic approach note pattern, 1 to 7 to 1), an arpeggio to the 7th, and then a single chromatic approach note that leads to the 5th of the new chord change on beat 1 of the next measure. Next, an arpeggiation that outlines the guide tone (7 to 3 in a ii-V), and then a 3-note chromatic approach note pattern (one half step above, two below) that leads to the 5th of the next chord in beat 1 of the next measure.

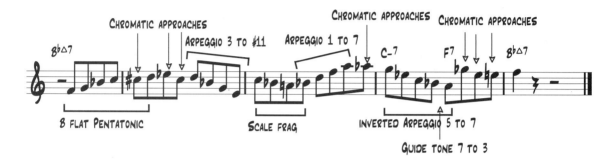

So this is how chromatic approach notes get used in an actual solo—these are chromatic approach notes in action.

Chromatic Approach Notes in 6 Steps

How do we work on integrating them into our playing and practice?
The best distillation of chromatic approach notes that I have seen is from Charlie Banacos, the legendary Boston teacher and pianist. He starts with the 12 combinations of 1 and 2 notes approaching a target pitch.

Please notice that there are other possible combinations of these pitches—for example, B, Bb, C—but in this case the chromatic pitches aren't all moving by half step in the direction of the target note. All the examples above move by half step in the direction of middle C.

1. Practice the above patterns and then learn them transposed to each of the 12 tones. You should be able to play each of the 12 patterns aiming at any target note.

2. This step is where things get interesting. How do chromatic approach note patterns function? In the Bud Powell example above, Bud builds his solo from common elements—scale fragments and arpeggios—and then adds chromatic approach notes to create interest and stress certain notes and to cause those notes to fall on strong beats. (Bud does these things simultaneously, of course. In order to take these sorts of lines apart and understand what is going on, though, it is helpful to think of chromatic approach note patterns as something that is added to the other harmonic material). So: let's take the scale fragment 1 2 3 5. Insert an approach note pattern before each note. Try all of the different possible patterns. Maybe you get something like this:

Work with it a little more. Try leaving some of the tones "unapproached." Keep a record of some of your favorite lines that you derive this way. Practice them over different chords. (The above scale 1 2 3 5 fragment can be part of a Bb major scale and it also could be part of any of the modes of that scale: C Dorian, D Phrygian, etc. It also could be part of the F and Eb scales and their modes and Eb melodic minor and its modes among others, so you can see that familiarity with this small scale fragment could have applications over a lot of different chords).

3. Try building lines using patterns other than 1 2 3 5. Try 1 3 5 7. Try using the chord tones of "difficult chords"—chords you are less familiar with. For example, work out the patterns to chord tones of a Ab-7b5, or B-Ma7. Here are a few more examples to help you on your way with this.

4. Okay, back to chromatic approach notes. One of the great things about chromatic approach notes is that they give you a lot of ammunition. I can keep adding approach note patterns to scale fragments and arpeggios, and this will generate lots of lines over any chord. **(CD EXAMPLE 5 chromatic approach note patterns, scale fragments and arpeggios over G-7)**

After working on a few hard keys, take a particular chord quality (for example, minor 7ths), and spend a long time playing scale fragments and scales and combining these with different chromatic approach note patterns. Do it slowly, letting your ear help you make meaningful choices. Go around the circle of fifths or randomly from key to key. Then move to another quality and start going around to different keys again, until you have worked on major 7ths in all keys. Try all of the different chord qualities: major 7, minor 7ths, dominant 7ths, minor7 b5, diminished 7ths, dominant 7sus4 chords, minor major 7ths.

5. After you have spent a fair amount of time on this, try writing down a few lines over each chord type. Try to use all of the different chromatic approach note patterns at some point in these lines.

6. Transpose the above lines by ear into all twelve keys.

Practice tip #10
Hard keys

Playing in hard or unfamiliar keys is extremely useful. For one thing, your hand hasn't been habituated to playing in these keys so you can use them as ear-training aids. Your ears have to tell your fingers what to play, since muscle memory isn't working for you. When trying to get greater fluency in these keys, chromatic approach notes are helpful because the problem isn't always that you don't know the scale of a difficult key, sometimes the problem is that you don't the notes that AREN'T in the scale in that key. That sounds complicated. What I mean is, if you are playing a Ab-7b5 it's as important to know what to do with notes like Eb, F natural and G natural as it is to know the notes of the Ab Locrian scale. Getting to know the "wrong notes" in the scale is actually a little easier than getting to know the "right notes" because there are less of them. There are usually 5. And of course, some are more wrong than others. Perhaps most importantly, knowing what notes aren't in the scale helps you to take in the harmonic universe of this less familiar key. It's a little bit like that Star Trek sensor shirt—you have to have a sense of how all twelve notes function in the key even if you aren't using all of them all the time.

So I sometimes tell my students that pianists are lucky that the keys look so different as you go around the circle of 5ths. (Lucky us that Gb and B are hard to play in! Students,

CHROMATIC APPROACH NOTE WRAP UP

1 Practice the 12 combinations of 1 and 2 approach notes to a target note in all keys.

2 Practice (start very slowly and out of time) adding the above approach note combinations to scale fragments: 1 2 3 5 in a few keys.

3 Practice adding approach note patterns to the chord tones (1 3 5 7) of a few different sevenths (in familiar keys).

4 Use chromatic approach notes to get to know some chords you are less familiar with, chords in "harder" keys.

5 Write down some of your favorite patterns, to make 2- or 4-bar licks constructed of chord tones and the chromatic patterns that precede them.

6 Construct such a lick for each chord quality. Write it down and transpose it around the circle of 5ths to all keys.

Guide Tones

There is one more approach that I want to talk about before moving on to work on some specific tunes. Guide tones are lines of longer rhythmic values (usually half notes or whole notes) that outline the harmony of a chord progression. The most common sort of guide tone line is one that follows a ii-7 V7 progression, moving from the 7th on the ii chord to the 3rd of the V chord. But I want to talk about guide tone lines in a more general sense than this, meaning any longer, slower line that moves predominantly by half or whole steps through a set of chord changes. This goes back to something we talked about a bit earlier—that the sound of outlining or spelling the basic harmony of the tune comes from paying attention to the notes that change moving from chord to chord. Focusing on common tone relationships (meaning the notes that are the same between chords) tends to erase the sense of difference between chords and as such can be extremely useful. It is impossible to do entirely one thing or the other. Every guide tone line tends to be a mix of notes that change chord to chord and notes that don't change. But at least in the early stages of working on improvising over chord changes, I think it is probably most useful to seek out new notes as they become available on each new chord change.

Tip #10 continued

of course, tend not to see it that way.) It lets you put your ears to work in a very direct way. I am told that Jim Hall sometimes tunes his guitar randomly to break up finger-ing patterns and to force himself to examine how much of his playing is ear driven and how much is derived from muscle memory. In the same way, we can switch to Gb or A major and be on less familiar terrain.

Guide Tone Lines Can Be Used in Several Ways

1. As a way of practicing at faster tempos. If I want to practice playing over "Giant Steps" at a fast tempo, I can still keep the tempo up if I play fewer, longer notes. This is more useful than it sounds. What's the problem with "Giant Steps"? Switching chords quickly. If I am playing half notes I am still practicing switching chord scales quickly, because each half note is on a new chord scale even though I am only playing one note of the scale. I have to be aware of the options open to me in each new scale situation as I switch from one scale to the other. So, even though I am not playing a lot of notes, I am getting familiar with all of the scale options available to me. Or, in other words, when I am working on these longer rhythmic values, I am still spending the same amount of time on each chord change as I am when I am playing 8th notes, whatever tempo I am playing; the chords are flying by at the same rate however many notes I choose to play on each one. Therefore, playing many, many guide tone lines through a set of chord changes will help me familiarize myself with these shifting chord scales at a fast tempo, and it offers another option to always slowing down the tempo to work on scales. At some point, we are going to have to work on fast tempos at the speed they really are. It's essential if I am ever going to be comfortable soloing on a difficult tune fast.

2. As a sort of underpinning or structure buried in the 8th note lines that I am playing. We don't have a lot of quotes from Charlie Parker as to what methods he employed in his own practicing, but one thing I've heard attributed to him is that he tried to create lines that used the upper parts of the chords as hinge notes for his solos. What he meant by this, I believe, is that the notes that are the targets of his lines, often notes around which he ornamented or that are preceded by chromatic approach notes, form a kind of guide tone line that emphasizes chord tensions. So, here is a method that we can employ in our own practicing.

Guide Tones in 4 Steps

1. Returning to our blues in Bb: write a line of all whole notes over the form. Try to move mostly by half step or whole step. Try to emphasize the notes that differ from chord to chord. try to hit interesting notes in this line, such as #11ths, 9ths and 13ths. Here's mine:

Writing out the line helps you understand the process of improvising these sorts of lines. Practice improvising many lines like the one above.

2. Also, practice singing these lines while playing the chords or roots of the chords.

3. Pick a particular line that you like. Play the line many times. If possible sing the line while you add notes to it. Perhaps something like this will emerge:

Perhaps something better. **(CD EXAMPLE 6: Guide Tone over Bb Blues; CD EXAMPLE 7: Embellishing the guide tone line over Bb Blues)** The point is that once you start ornamenting your guide tone line, the shape of the solos is constrained by the line you are working with. Even as you obscure the line more and more, a little of its structure remains and that gives your solo a shape that is very musical. Practicing this way will lead you to being aware of the underlying shape of lines when you are improvising with shorter rhythmic values.

4. Repeat steps 1 to 3 many times, composing new guide tone lines, learning them and practicing using them as an underlying structure for your solos.

G U I D E   T O N E   W R A P - U P

1 Compose several guide tone lines over the blues progression.
2 Improvise many guide tone lines over the blues progression.
3 Repeat step 2, singing.
4 Pick a line you like and memorize it.
5 Practice ornamenting that line, adding notes and melodic embellishment.

Well, that pretty much covers our discussion of ways to improve your ability to make lines on chord changes. We will revisit these techniques when we start working on tunes, but in general you should already have a lot of ideas of ways that you can strengthen your lines by trying different ways of attacking scales, arpeggios, chromatic approach notes and guide tone lines. You can apply these approaches to any tune that you are working on. As we go, I envision that you are developing a battery of methods to apply to your practice in different situations that you will encounter. So don't forget these approaches! Make these a part of your daily practicing in a quasi-religious way, adapting them to your own way of thinking chord practicing.

CHAPTER 4: *"Body and Soul" – A Great Yet In Many Ways Typical, Standard Tune*

Maybe you skipped to get to this chapter and maybe you've worked diligently on each page of this book to get here, but in either case, from here on out you must throw yourself into practicing body and soul. (Okay, that was pretty corny, but let's continue.)

"Jazz standards," "Tin Pan Alley" tunes or songs from the "Great American Songbook" are all names for a repertoire of 20th century American popular music that jazz musicians still play. Songwriters like Jimmy Van Heusen, George Gershwin, Cole Porter, Irving Berlin, Richard Rodgers, Jerome Kern, Harold Arlen, Alec Wilder, Leonard Bernstein, Duke Ellington and hundreds of others have created an extensive body of work that, despite stylistic differences from composer to composer, has many features in common.

"Body and Soul" is a fairly typical example. It's 32 bars long, which is the most common length for a standard tune. It has the most common form for a standard, AABA. (The next most common form is ABAC found in such tunes as "My Romance," "Green Dolphin Street" and "Days of Wine and Roses.") (These forms should not be confused with ABBA forms like "Fernando" or "Money, Money, Money." Sorry). In an AABA tune the first 8-bar phrase (A) is repeated (usually with a slightly different ending the second time), then followed by a different 8-bar phrase (B, also known as "the Bridge") that leads back to the first phrase (A), usually ending with the second A's ending. Harmonically, the chord progression of "Body and Soul" is mostly based on ii-7 V7 I and diatonic harmony in the key of Db with modulations to D major and C major in the bridge. A sections that are mostly diatonic with bridges that modulate a lot is a very common harmonic plan for a standard (although a bridge that starts by modulating to the bII degree is pretty unusual) and there are a lot of standards that work this way ("Cherokee," "When Sunny Gets Blue," "I Can't Get Started" and "Chelsea Bridge," to name a few).

(See example, next page)

Practice tip #11
The appeal of standards

So why do we still play standards? Certainly, we play them because we like them and they have memorable melodies, good lyrics, etc. How important playing standards is varies from individual musician to musician. There are some jazz musicians who play almost entirely original music, rarely playing standards. Some musicians settle on playing original music after years of playing standards, like John Coltrane. Some musicians play only standards their whole careers and some musicians return to standards after years of playing only original music, most notably Keith Jarrett, who after performing his own compositions with his quartets, has returned to playing almost exclusively standards with his trio. Jarrett has said that standards give him a sense of freedom because their structures are so familiar to him and his bandmates. When he first decided to play standards with Jack DeJohnette and Gary Peacock, Keith Jarrett said, "Let's not worry about the material. And it created a kind of freedom, I think, for all of us, that we've never had before."

Of course, to get to the point where you can forget everything and play so freely over standards, you have to spend some time studying and playing them.

These tunes are lasting because there is something iconic about them, their melodies and harmonic progressions. When jazz musicians write tunes, they tend to make the harmony more complex than the harmony of standards. Jazz musicians' originals are, in a sense, already reharmonized. The hip chords have already been added to them. Standards are like blank slates, you can add lots of interesting reharmonizations or unusual voicings because the harmonic material is more basic.

Of course, there are lots of exceptions to this—musicians' tunes that use a standard-like harmonic vocabulary (such as those by Duke

BODY AND SOUL

MUSIC BY JOHNNY GREEN

One of the reasons that I picked this tune is because it has a strong and interesting melody, but the melody doesn't move SO much that it is difficult to make voicings with the melody as the top note on the piano. Generally speaking, melodies that move in 8th notes (like bebop heads, but also tunes like "Honeysuckle Rose" and "It Could Happen to You") present certain obstacles to arranging for the piano. But more on that later.

The other reason I picked "Body and Soul" is because it is one of the greatest and most played standards and every young musician eventually encounters this tune. It's been recorded by hundreds of jazz musicians in all styles, from Coleman Hawkins, Billie Holiday and Art Tatum to Freddie Hubbard, Johnny Griffin, Wes Montgomery, Stan Getz, John Coltrane, Keith Jarrett and Archie Shepp.

Tip #11 continued

Ellington) and standards that have complex and unusual progressions, although a lot of the songs from this second category get simplified over time, stripped of the particularities of their broadway arrangements by being played repeatedly.

Knowing standards well teaches you something about how tunes work, about turnarounds and modulations, the theoretical components that are put together in these and other songs.

One habitual problem with young musicians is that they don't know enough tunes and the thinness of their repertoire keeps them from being flexible in situations where

By saying that this song is typical, I don't mean to put the tune down, or imply that there is nothing special about this particular tune. Cabaret musicians (especially) wax poetic about the Great American Songbook and there is a lot of controversy (among people who care about this sort of thing) about how much you can do to a standard before you've simply gone too far and obliterated some of the song's important defining qualities. This is something that I personally am not all that interested in (although if you go too far in my reharmonization class, I'll make you transcribe the entire recorded work of Michael Feinstein). You can't legislate taste and what you do with these tunes is ultimately up to you. My intention is to get you to see the many similarities in these tunes so that you can learn them faster and play them better.

Melody

I've done a lot of clinics with the great saxophone player Dick Oatts, and at some point he'll talk about playing the melody. Improvising over a song is about playing lines over the chord changes, and that is one of the structures that a soloist uses when he or she solos, but the melody is of equal if not greater importance to playing on the song. How often does someone come up to you and say, "Hey, do you know this song? Here are the roots of the chord changes," and then they sing the roots to you. If someone wants to know if you know the song, he'll sing the melody to you. I've heard a lot of jam sessions, where three or four horn players basically beat the heck out of the melody in unison for a chorus and then start blowing for uncountably many choruses over the chord changes. You don't hear much from the melody until they drag it out for another beating as a prerequisite to blowing over turnarounds at the end of the tune. If this is what you are after, then you might as well dispense with the melody altogether.

And yet some of our most profound associations with music are melodies of songs. When I was in high school I got hooked on Coltrane's Crescent record, and I used to listen to Trane playing the melody of "Lonnie's Lament" over and over and it would bring tears to my

Tip #11continued

someone is calling tunes without music.

I'm here to help. Here are 55 essential standards that you should know and the keys they are most often played in. Are there others that are equally important as the tunes on this list? Quite possibly, but this is a place to start. In this list, I am only including standards, not common tunes written by jazz musicians (except where the jazz musician has written a standard-type tune. The boundaries may get a little fuzzy but the big picture is clear more or less). You should know tunes like "Stablemates," "Song for My Father" and "Moment's Notice," but since they aren't standards, I'm not including them in this list.

"Bye Bye Blackbird"	F
"Green Dolphin Street"	C, Eb
"Night And Day"	C, Eb
"Softly As In A Morning Sunrise"	C-
"Secret Love"	Eb
"Body and Soul"	Db
"It Could Happen To You"	Eb
"All The Things You Are"	Ab
"Just In Time"	Bb
"You Don't Know What Love Is"	F-
"If I Should Lose You"	G-
"Love For Sale"	Bb-
"Invitation"	C-/Eb
"I Thought About You"	F
"My Funny Valentine"	C-
"Jitterbug Waltz"	Eb, Db
"Emily"	C
"All Of Me"	C, F
"All Of You"	Eb
"What Is This Thing Called Love"	C
"Alone Together"	D-
"Autumn Leaves"	Bb/G-
"Cherokee"	Bb
"Caravan"	F-
"Days of Wine and Roses"	F
"Darn That Dream"	G
"Embraceable You"	Eb, G
"Falling In Love With Love"	Bb
"Triste"	Bb, A
"Girl From Ipanema"	F
"Corcovado"	C
"Wave"	D
"Lady Bird"	C
"Speak Low"	F

eyes. Miles playing "It Never Entered my Mind," Keith Jarrett on "Old Folks," Louis Armstrong singing "Azalea," Bill Evans on "Never Let me Go," Sonny Rollins playing "Namely You," Trane with Johnny Hartman playing the melody on "My One and Only Love," Monk on "Just a Gigolo." Of course the list goes on and on—singers, horn players, pianists—the important thing to remember is that the improvising starts with the downbeat of the song, not after the melody is over so we can get to the blowing.

I guess I have a little pet peeve with (some) pianists on this score. Part of the problem is with the instrument itself. If you work out complex arrangements of the melody with specific voicings and kicks for the band, you might have difficulty playing the melody more than one way. Some of this is stylistic preference, of course, and you might want the sound of a piano trio imitating a big band with set kicks and complex chordal arrangements. On the other hand, there's Monk, someone who worked on the melody the whole time he was playing the song. He was extremely orchestral and pianistic, but kept reworking the melody, making subtle changes that allowed it to feel like a living lyrical thing. I like to see the melody evolve over the course of a tune so that the head out is different from the head in. I also like the feeling of phrasing the melody and varying that phrasing and the ornamentation of the melody in the moment as it occurs to you.

Tip #11 continued	
"Just Friends"	G, F
"Stella By Starlight"	Bb, G
"Have You Met Miss Jones"	F
"I Got Rhythm"	Bb
"Chelsea Bridge"	Db
"Honeysuckle Rose"	F, Bb
"I Love You"	F
"If I Were A Bell"	F
"I'll Remember April"	G
"In A Sentimental Mood"	F/D-
"I'm Old Fashioned"	C
"Like Someone in Love"	Eb, Ab
"My One And Only Love"	C
"My Shining Hour"	Eb, C
"Prelude To A Kiss"	C
"Star Eyes"	Eb
"There Is No Greater Love"	Bb
"There Will Never Be Another You"	Eb
"What's New"	C
"Yesterdays"	D-
"Sophisticated Lady"	Ab
"Summertime"	A-

Practicing the Melody

Sing it. Learn the words. I don't always know the words of every standard tune that I play, but I always know the words to an A section, the words of the first and second endings, the bridge. And if I don't know the words exactly, I know the rhythm of the words. (And it would be better to know all the words exactly, but we're all fallible.) It's okay to change the melody, but if you play it in such a way that convinces me that you have learned it incorrectly, or that you have learned someone else's ornamentation as if that is the real melody of the tune, then that isn't okay. It just sounds wrong to people who know the melody, and I think there is something fishy that gets communicated even to people who don't know the melody. Often the part of the melody that young instrumentalists (and vocalists) skip over is the part of the tune that is most colorful or chromatic, replacing those parts with something diatonic and bland. Again, it is best to know the words of the song, learn them if you can, but at least if you know "You are the promised kiss of springtime that makes the lonely winter dah dah" You won't screw up the song rhythms by playing "You are the promised kiss of springtime that makes the lonely winter dah dah dah" or " makes the lonely winter dah" ("seem long," if I am not mistaken).

This point was brought home to me recently. I was in Japan listening to a good young tenor player, and he was playing some ballad, "Polka Dots and Moonbeams," I think. (You can add that to the above list if you want, it's usually in F). He was playing the melody and embroidering it with ornamental stuff, little lines and ideas that he played in the holes, and something just sounded wrong to me. It wasn't until they went on a break and we started to talk that I realized the problem: his English wasn't very good. The rhythms of the melody as he was playing it weren't lining up with the speech rhythms of the lyrics in English. In this song, the first phrase of the melody ends with the line "in a garden" and later is rhymed at the end of the next phrase with "beg your pardon," but this sax player ended these phrases with a long note ("in a gaaar," "beg your paaar") and it sounded wrong.

Of course, this experience cuts both ways. Recently I was transcribing several tunes from an Elis Regina recording (a great Brazilian singer) and had a lot of trouble deciding how to write the melody. Which of the rhythms were "the melody"? She phrased it differently each time and the second chorus of the song had different rhythms because the words were different. That particular problem can happen in any language, but some of my difficulties with these rhythms clearly had to do with the fact that they weren't in English, where the rhythmic signature of the words is imprinted in me through my knowledge of the language. Sometimes its as simple as not knowing which syllable in a word is stressed. The difficulties of getting the rhythm of words that are in a language you don't speak are surmountable, but it does make things more difficult, and jazz players who are not native speakers of English need to be aware of the issue when playing standards.

Actually there is a little zen in the issue of knowing the melody of the song and not playing it exactly. I know, when I hear Miles play a ballad, that he knows the melody of the song no matter how much he deviates from it (and sometimes he deviates a great deal). It's like looking at a Matisse—I remember seeing a series of studies he did in preparation for a painting in which he started with a completely accurate realistic portrait of a woman and then gradually abstracted it until he got to his desired result. The exact likeness was the starting point for the final abstract painting, and something of that original likeness was buried in the final abstract product.

So sing the melody. Play it. Play it for many many choruses. First play it as exactly as you can. Could you write it down perfectly, without any questions about any notes in the melody line, knowing how each phrase begins and ends, whether there are pickups to start the phrase and all of those other details? Next try phrasing the melody a little more loosely. Can you keep the pitches exactly but change the way you phrase them each time you play? When you feel comfortable with this, start to embellish the melody more. Can you play lines in the "holes" of the melody, the long notes where the melody line is holding at the end of a phrase? As you start to play the melody, think about the ways you could personalize it to make it more like a great singer singing this song. Play it in many keys. Listen to different instrumentalists play the melody. How does Duke phrase it? How does Keith Jarrett phrase it? How do Sarah Vaughn, Carmen McRae and Louis Armstrong phrase it? And then, how do you phrase it, and eventually, how are you going to phrase it today, since every time you play the melody the phrasing can be new and fresh. **(CD EXAMPLE 8: Improvising around the melody on Body and Soul; CD EXAMPLE 9: Dick Oatts improvising around the melody on Body and Soul)**

When I first hit on this idea for practicing I could easily spend 30 minutes just playing variations of a melody, over and over, changing things subtly. As I started to deviate a little more from the melody, I would try to improvise counterlines and responses to the melody in the holes of the melody, ornamenting it. Gradually increasing the amount of ornamentation, eventually the line between ornamenting and playing a solo gets blurry. Doing this helped free up my sense of what playing the melody means, and helped me to begin an improvisation at the beginning of the song instead of at the top of the solo chorus.

Exploring Voicings: Piano for Non-Pianists

This book is written from the perspective of a pianist. About 85 percent of it is understandable and applicable to work on any instrument and about 15 percent of the material addresses piano players' problems. Some of that material will probably only be interesting to pianists. Still, piano skills are extremely important for all jazz musicians to develop. Understanding the piano, even on a relatively basic level, gives you the ability to understand principles of harmony that you can't master on an instrument that can only play one note at a time. Knowing the keyboard gives you the ability to visualize harmony and allows you to explore chord sounds, develop your ear and understand the harmonic context that your soloing on a single line instrument fits into.

Most great horn players and many drummers and bassists are fine pianists. I remember a jam session years ago with Bill Stewart and Chris Potter. I left the room to answer the phone and when I hung up, I could hear the two of them playing Wayne Shorter's "Nefertiti" together. I knew Chris was an excellent piano player, but was surprised to see Bill at the piano and Chris playing drums.

Let's talk about playing voicings. I've seen a lot of different approaches to working on piano voicings for beginners and they are all good. What I mean by that is that students are usually told to use a particular voicing, often one that stresses voice leading so that the left hand doesn't have to move a lot. There are a lot of good places to use these kinds of voicings. Or students might be told to play the root and seventh in the left hand and work around that, and that voicing is good too, and the resulting "spread voicings" with 1 and 7 in the left hand are good to know and get used by a lot of great pianists. Or someone might teach you to play a non-root voicing in the left hand built around the 3rd and the 7th of the chord that has good voice leading between the ii-7 and the V7 of a ii-V-I progression. You know, that's a good voicing too!

You can find examples of great pianists using all of these voicings. The important thing is (eventually) to be able to think of all of the available voicings occurring simultaneously on the piano. If I have the sense of what voicings are available to me in different parts of the instrument, I can pick whatever I need in the moment. So let's look at the thinking around all of the voicings and come up with principles that allow you to understand typical voicings and move beyond that to invent your own.

If all of the piano players and piano records were destroyed tomorrow (that would be a good start—no, that's a lawyer joke, I think) we could still construct the world of jazz voicings pretty easily by looking at the piano and listening to what the various registers sound like. The extreme bottom of the piano is more of an effect than a functional harmonic part of the instrument. About an octave up is where notes start to feel like they have a real bass function. In this range of the piano, close intervals tend to sound muddy, so it is more usual to find either single bass notes or wide intervals such as octaves, 9ths and 10ths. A little higher up and you might see intervals of a 7th—you start to see them around here, but this is toward the bottom of the 7th's range because of its dissonance. The most common exception to these large intervals in the bass register is the 5th, which has an open pure sound that doesn't get muddy in the lower registers. (Keep in mind, muddiness might be something that you want to employ in your voicings—but, if so, you are going to want to be sensitive to how much of it you can use. Also, different pianos have muddier or clearer low registers. A very good concert grand gives you options in the low registers that aren't usable on other smaller instruments. Still, the general tendencies we are discussing hold true in most situations.)

Now, moving up the piano to the octave below middle C, this is where intervals can get closer—minor 2nds are fine here, although more common a 5th below middle C than an octave below. This is where we tend to put the meat of the chord, again not always, but as a tendency it holds true. Roots, 3rds and 7ths define most chords (by which I mean, they are the essential defining notes of the chord since they tell you what sort of 7th it is and whether the chord is major or minor) and you often see the 3rds and 7ths of the chords in this range of the piano. Tensions also appear here, but usually mixed with chord tones. Again, although it is a rule that is often broken to beautiful effect, chord tones are more often below tensions in the voicing than the other way around. Violating this rule will make your voicings sound a bit less normal, which can be good or bad.

Generally speaking, in the notes around the middle C range of the piano you start to see the lower end of the range of the melody. Any size interval works here and you find more tensions along with chord tones the further up the instrument you go. An octave above middle C is the middle high range of the melody, and an octave above that would be towards the top range of the melody in common situations. The range above an octave above middle C is quite high. Often melodies up there are reinforced with doubling the note an octave below, although a solo line (or line harmonized in 3rds) high up the piano has a flute-like quality that can be used in situations where that sound is desired—I am thinking of Bossa Nova arrangements, but of course the examples of this technique are many and varied in style.

We can add to our voicing concept by thinking of a few simple rules regarding voicings. Even spacing of the notes in voicings that cover a large range on the piano tends to make large resonant-sounding chords. Voicings that have a lot of smaller intervals in them (clusters) have a distinctive "crunchy" sound. The presence of smaller intervals in a voicing are the "crunches" that give a lot of voicings their distinctive color, their sound. Of course, these two types of voicings overlap a great deal—you can have wide voicings that cover a lot of space on the piano that have a crunchy minor second imbedded in the chord.

And that's most of what you need to know to make voicings. Basically, what I do as a pianist is to stack intervals. I have to develop an interest in what intervals sound like stacked one on top of the other. What do two 4ths sound like? How about a 4th and a major 2nd? These interval stacks are the materials with which I can create a wide range of chord colors.

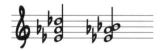

Let's take the first chord of "Body and Soul," Eb -7. I can think about voicing this chord in many ways:

1. I can think about the bass note, way down on the piano, and I can play it or not.
2. How about 1 and 7 in the left hand starting in the octave below the octave below middle C? This is the lower end of where 1 and 7 sounds good on a lot of pianos, but it's a possibility.
3. How about stacking a single interval? Like 5ths. In the bass this gives me 1, 5 and 9. If I start another stack of 5ths starting on the minor 3rd next to the 9th (below middle C) I can have the b3, b7 and natural 11—a common but lovely open sounding voicing with one crunch in it. (Some of the elements that make this voicing sound unique are the stacked 5ths, the half step, the 9th below the 3rd and the 11th on top of the chord).

4. 4ths are also very stackable. If I start an octave up from the last example on the Eb below middle C with: Eb Ab Db Gb and Bb, I get three 4ths with a 3rd on top: the famous voicing Bill Evans uses on Miles Davis's "So What."

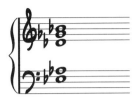

5. The intervals that I choose to stack are dependent on the chord tones and tensions that are available to me. In the above situation if I wanted to keep stacking 4ths instead of putting a 3rd on top, I couldn't do it—the next 4th after the Gb gives me a B, making the chord an Eb-7b6, which might be more than I want for the situation. (It's a lovely sound, but usually in a tune that is very strongly Db major you aren't going to expect to find B naturals, especially on the first chord.) The note a 4th above the B, E natural or b9 (a note not considered to be an available tension on a minor 7th), is going to sound so dissonant that it's rarely chosen unless you want this very dissonant sound.

6. Let's dig into this interval idea more fully. One way to build interesting voicings is to write down the chord scale, like this:

Eb F Gb Ab Bb C Db

Now I choose a note that I think would be an interesting starting place for my voicing let's say F below middle C. I'll add a 5th above, so I have this sort of open large interval at the bottom of the voicing. (All of these judgments are subjective—there is no right and wrong way to build this chord.) Also I've started with two tensions, a 9th and a 13th at the bottom of my voicing, so already I've taken an unusual tack.

Now I erase the notes I've used from my chord scale, and what remains looks like this:

Eb Gb Ab Bb Db

Let's put the Db next to the C for a crunch in the middle of this voicing. Now another larger interval—a Gb, since we want to make sure we get the minor 3rd into the chord and to get the sound of the 4th.

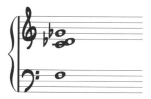

It's already a great sounding voicing and of course I could stop there.

We have these notes remaining in the scale:

Eb Ab Bb

Eb is implied in this case—we can play it underneath the whole voicing when we are done. Let's add the Ab next to the Gb. Now I could put the Bb next to the Ab, or I could leave it off. As I said, I could have stopped anywhere during this process whenever I had a sound that I liked. Another possibility is to put the Bb up an octave and I'll hear this unusual space in the chord. Okay, here's the voicing I built: (and you can add the root Eb underneath the chord to hear it as an Eb-7).

It's unusual because of the spaces in it, and it's unusual because it starts on a 9th and then has a 13th and then the chord tones that you often find lower in the voicing. I can also hear the prominence of 4ths and 5ths in this voicing.

I can build a nearly infinite number of voicings in this way. And I can challenge myself to find voicings that I haven't used before. Leaving chord tones out effects the sound of the voicing (see Practice tip #12). I can usually leave out the 5th pretty easily, but how about if I leave out the 3 or the 7? These chords have a sort of unfinished quality that can be very beautiful. Working with this sort of approach allows me to find new voicings.

Things to keep in mind when working on voicings

1 Don't double root usually.
2 Include 3 and 7 usually (for normal sounding versions of the chords).
3 Look for interesting intervals and spaces between the notes.
4 Have an even spread of notes over the range of the chord unless you want a more angular unfinished sound.
5 Look at all the possibilities—if you are playing a 5, what about replacing it with the #11 or the 13th? If you are doubling the 3rd, why not add a 9th or an 11th instead?
    Make sure that you check all of the altered possibilities on dominant 7th chords—b9, natural 9 and #9, #11, b13 and natural 13.

So we've looked at how to make some nice and potentially unusual voicings for the first chord of "Body and Soul." The next step I'd like you to do on your own: take the chord scale of each chord in the A section of this tune and work through the same process that we just finished with the Eb-7. Write down your favorite voicings. Which of them are most interesting to you? Transpose a few of them (or all of them if it interests you) around the circle of 5ths. This is the beginning of building your own repertoire of chord voicings.

Now let's backtrack a little and work on something that is in some ways less complicated theoretically, but extremely useful for all instrumentalists and an even more essential skill for vocalists: voicing the melody.

Tip #12 continued
you find voicings faster. Also, the more you use a particular chord, the more likely it is to become part of your vocabulary. Eventually, your personal chord vocabulary has a lot to do with your voice as a pianist, composer or arranger.

Practice tip #13
Memorizing chord changes

I was teaching at a summer jazz camp and had a student in his 50s who had come to work on his playing. He was a good guitarist—a school principal in his day-job life—and I had asked him to memorize the chord changes to the tune that we were working on in the "combo" session. (Okay, this is an aside here, but I can't stand the word "combo." Why does every jazz camp use that? I mean, jazz can seem far enough removed from the current social and musical world without using words like "combo." Incidentally, I'm not all that crazy about the word "improv" either. I can't picture Coltrane talking about the improv section of "A Love Supreme" as played by his combo. Okay, that's not exactly a practice tip; I just wanted to get it off my chest.) Anyway, he said that he found memorizing tunes extremely difficult to do and that this problem had really dogged his playing over the years. I told him that I could get him to memorize any tune in 5 minutes. "No way," he gasped. "Way," I replied.

It's not really that hard to do. The principal's problem was that all the chords had the same value to him and that he wasn't looking for common cadences and ii-V's or thinking in a key, he was just looking at the chords on the page in front of him and trying to remember all of them as a kind of random arrangement, like memorizing numbers out of the phone book. We were working on "You Don't Know What Love Is" and I asked him what key the tune was in. "Um...F-, I think." He said. Okay, here is the tune in F- (the I chord), then the vi-7b5 (optional) and ii-7b5 V7 to i- up a half step and then it pauses

Voicing the Melody in Three Steps

1. Play 1 and 7 in the left hand. Play the melody in the right hand. Now look at the space between the thumb of your left hand and the melody in your right hand. If the melody is not a 3rd of the chord, add the 3rd in this space if possible (playing the chord on the downbeat of each chord change, so usually on 1 and 3, but in a few of the bars that have four chord changes in them, you'll have to play a new voicing on each beat of the measure). Be able to play the whole song in this fashion.

2. Return your focus to the space between the thumb in the left hand and the melody. Maybe you've added a 3rd (although there are a few places in this song where the melody lands on the 3rd of the chord, so in those spots you don't need to add 3rds to the voicings and you are are playing just 3 notes). What other notes can you add? Don't double the root. What about the 9th? the 5th? the 13th? the 11th? Choose the notes that sound like the best choice to you and move on. Once you have settled on a voicing for each chord, make sure that you remember these voicings well enough to be able to play through your whole arrangement in time.

3. Play your version of the song. Where are the voicings that you don't like? Try to figure out what it is about these chords that doesn't please you. Are they too boxy? Is the melody overwhelmed by a particular voicing? Or does the voicing feel too small? Try some simple ways of rectifying this:

a. Try not to have all the voices in your chords change at the same time. Even though we are working on this tune in a very vertical way, you can break up the chords a little. When all the notes in both hands move in lock step (like a beginning pinball player that always moves both flippers in unison), the result is blocky and a little bit unmusical.

b. You can place a voicing at a different place in the measure so that you are harmonizing a note in the melody line other than whatever falls on beats 1 and 3. For example, play the first chord on the "and" of 1 in the first measure and the chord will fall under the first note of the melody, the Eb, but played at another part of the measure a different note will be emphasized. You can still play the root of the chord on beat one, with the rest of the chord occurring later. Delaying the point where the chord voicing falls will have the effect of accenting a different melody note. What notes in the melody should you harmonize? In this tune, where there are 8th notes you have several choices. You can harmonize each note, you can play the notes as a line without harmonizing them, or you can add a counterline underneath the note.

Tip #13 continued

you'll remember it again. You'll forget a few details now and then and you'll have to refresh your memory (wait, where does the bridge go again? Oh yeah, the bIII major...) and then you'll have it. But only if you stop reading it out of a book.

"Giant Steps"? Bmaj7 up a minor third to a dominant that leads to G and then up another minor third to a dominant that leads to Eb. Whenever you are on a Maj chord for a whole bar the following ii-V always starts a tritone away in this tune so: A-7 to D7, Gmajor up a min 3rd to a dominant chord that leads to Eb then up a min 3rd to a dominant that leads to B for a bar. Tritone away ii-V to Eb for a bar. Tritone away ii-V to a G for a bar. Tritone away ii-V to a B for a bar. Tritone away ii-V to a Eb for a bar. Pattern is broken for the last ii-V that leads back to the B at the top. Clear! What could be simpler to memorize?

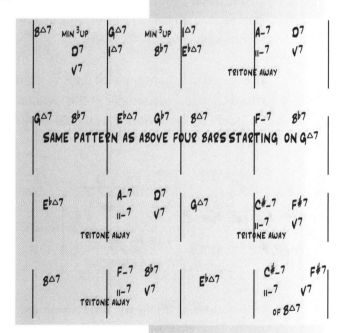

The counterline could move in the same rhythm (each note has a note a certain interval below it) or in a different rhythm (faster or slower rhythms than the melody). You can have more than one voice below the melody (either moving in the same rhythm, like block chords or as a held chord underneath the melody).

And yet I've seen students reading this tune for chorus after chorus. I almost never read changes while I am soloing. If it's a standard, I've usually heard it. If I've heard it and never played it, I might glance at the changes and get a sense of where we are going, but then I want to internalize the form as quickly as possible.

c. Are there some places where the registration will allow you to add notes in between the 1 and 7 of your left hand? Adding the 3rd or the 11th is a nice even sound in the left hand if the voicing isn't too low. If you add a voice in your left hand you can sometimes remove that voice from your right hand so as to make a prettier, more evenly spaced sound.

d. Are there some places where 1 and 5 or 1, 5 and 3 (or 10, up an octave from the 3rd) is a better left hand choice than 1 and 7?

e. Sometimes the sound of those roots can feel a little heavy. Try picking a few voicings and leaving the root out. Use 7 and 3 in your left hand, or try building a chord in the chord scale oriented manner discussed earlier. Also, for parts of the song where the melody is in 8th notes (measure 1 of the bridge for example), if you DO harmonize those notes with a counterline of some sort or some kind of parallel movement harmonizing below the melody—as discussed above in (b)—you can try leaving out the left hand entirely, playing just the harmonization of the line. (More on this later when we are talking about counterpoint and internal lines.) Or just play those lines freely, as single lines without left hand accompaniment.

f. In some situations the root doesn't need to move for every chord change. For example, in the sixth bar of the tune, the Eb7 and Eb-7 both work over the Bb in the bass from the chord before like this

In the above example, the Bb is a momentary pedal. It frees up the feeling of chord changes moving on the first beat of each measure.

g. Some places where you are struggling with coming up with the right voicing might work better with a simple reharmonization. Tritone substitutes offer a common solution to some difficult voicing choices. (Bar 6 might be one place to try this.)

Practice tip #14
Why memorizing chords is important, the deep structure of songs

When I am playing with a musician I haven't worked with before—this happens mostly with students—and they pull out a Real Book, I always ask if there is some other tune that they have memorized that we can play. Why? It's not because I am trying to vibe them, I am a really really nice guy. (I might be the nicest guy you'll ever meet, although I guess that depends on who you meet.) It's because if their head is buried in a book they're going to miss some things going on on the bandstand. But it's more than that. If they are reading it means that they haven't internalized the form of the song, and they are just responding to the changes as they come spontaneously, without a sense of what is coming a bar or two ahead, without a sense of which changes are crucially important and which could be left out. It's because they don't know that the changes in front of them are always an approximation of the platonic ideal of the change—the deep structure of the tune.

There is a great moment in an interview show that Marian McPartland did with Bill Evans where she asks him what is important for students to learn when they are working on a tune, and he says that first they should learn the harmonic structure of the tune. And Marian McPartland asks, you mean the chord changes? and Bill says, no—the structure of the tune. He goes on to explain that he means the harmonic map of the tune: where the modulations are, what chords are important, what chords might be replaced by a tritone or left out entirely, where the half cadences are and where the full cadences are. In the examples of changes that I gave above as shorthand for memorization, you can see the underlying structure of the song, so that if someone decides to change something—adding a ii to a V, using a tritone (for the bVI7 chords in "You Don't Know What Love is," you could

h. If you feel that there is too much parallel movement in your left hand, try using 1 and 3. This is another option to make the LH chord feel lighter and less blocky. It also makes for good voice leading in a lot of situations where 1 and 7 feels too thick and sort of claw-like, particularly for the V chord in a ii-V situation. (Again, bar 6 might be one place to try this.)

Try the above suggestions in the places where you aren't satisfied with your voicings and learn your new arrangement. To give you an idea, here is an arrangement of the melody using the above suggestions. **(CD EXAMPLE 10: Body and Soul, melody voiced according to the given rules)**

We have worked on the melody, as a singable living thing, and worked on voicing that melody in a few basic ways. Let's start dealing with soloing over the chord changes of the tune.

Soloing with a focus on the Ear (A 12 Step Program)

Let's re-familiarize ourselves with the form. Play the roots on 1 in each measure and play the melody (with minimal ornamentation). Make sure that you can do this without mistakes or faltering before you go on to the next step. Make sure this is memorized.

The next step to working on "Body and Soul" is to more fully internalize the form. So here is the shorthand analysis of the tune.

Db: ii-7 to V7/ii back to ii-7 to V7 to I Maj7 to IV7 then iii-7 to a half-step-down diminished 7th chord (functions kind of like a V7/ii) then ii-7 then a V7 and its related ii-7 chord of vi, that vi-7 becomes the ii in a ii-7 V7 of V, then ii- 7 V7 IMaj7, with a ii-7 V7 of ii back up to the top in the first ending. The second ending is I chord for two beats and then a ii-7 V7 to D major. The Bridge is D: IMaj7, ii-7, IMaj7 (first inversion) iv-7 and its related dominant, iii-7, V/ii-7, ii-7, V7, I Maj7. C: ii-7 V7 iii-7, biii diminished 7, ii-7 V7 I7, then a half-step-down dominant and another half-step-down dominant that leads back to the last A as a V7 of ii-7. And we're done.

Tip #14 continued

use the ii-7b6)—you'll catch it. Each set of chord changes for a tune is a realization of this underlying harmony, but none of the sets of chord changes are "right" per se. Since we are trying to get at the deep structure of the tune it's usually best expressed as the simplest way through the chord changes. (The Occam's razor of jazz theory—look it up.)

I had another somewhat illustrative experience on this score when I first moved to New York. I was playing a duo gig with a bassist that I had heard was a great player. I called a couple of tunes, "Yesterdays" or "I Thought About You," and he said he didn't know those tunes. So I went down the list of standards that I was playing at the time and he didn't know any of them. "You know, I thought this was more of an art gig," he said. " Last week I played here and we played all Ornette Coleman and Monk tunes. I know all of the Monk tunes, there are 77 of them." At the time I knew about 6 Monk tunes, the ones most people know, and so we played those. The thing is, when you are playing "Evidence," you are really playing "Just You, Just Me"; or when you are playing "In Walked Bud," you are playing "Blue Skies" (A sections); or when you are playing "Hackensack," you are playing "Lady Be Good"; and Monk knew that and Monk's bass players knew that. There's a great DVD of Monk in Europe with John Ore that is very illustrative of this. John Ore sounds great and very free in his approach to the chord changes, adding tritone substitutes and interpreting the harmony, as a bassist of his experience with standards would be able to. All of Monk's bassists play tritone reharmonizations and use all sorts of approaches that come from a knowledge of standards. So when I played the Monk tunes with this otherwise good bassist, he played them in a way that sounded kind of stiff to me, as if he didn't know all the ways he could make the tune feel loose, all the ways he could make the tune breathe harmonically. He was playing the changes, but he didn't know the deep structure of the song because he hadn't spent enough time

Whenever you are working on a new tune, memorize the chords by being able to say the form in a few sentences like we've done.

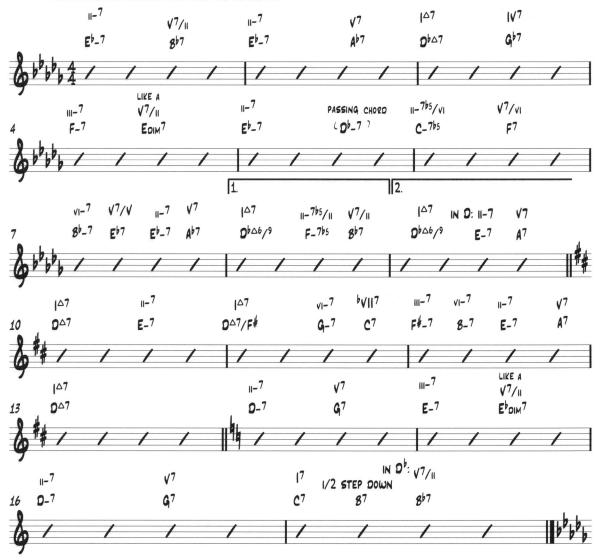

DC TO 2ND ENDING

Here's the next step: Learn the sound of the roots (whole notes) on the downbeats. This should become a second melody for you. Being able to hear the roots underneath your solo (whether you are playing them or not) is really important for soloing. For one thing, it keeps you from getting lost. So,

1 Play the roots alone. Sing the melody

2 Play the melody alone. Sing the roots.

3 Play any random note in the lower register, say, D. Make this the bass note of the first chord of "Body and Soul." Now play the rest of the roots, by ear, just trying to hear the intervals, not using math to transpose. (If you start

Tip #14 continued

with standards to understand that songs have deep structures and all of the details are up for negotiation. He was thinking of the song as a received set of chord changes, as "original compositions" that were too precious to mess around with much. I'd rather make subtle changes in the way the chords are played, reworking each chorus depending on what the content of the solo needs.

The fact is, that even when you are playing "Trinkle Tinkle" or "Round Midnight," you are playing tunes that, while not written on the changes of standard tunes, might as well have

on D, then the tune is in C, and the changes are D-7 A7 D-7 G7 CM7 F7 E-7, etc.)

4   Now let's play the melody with the roots. In this case, the first melody note is the same pitch as the root of the first chord, so play any octave and go from there. Pick a random pitch (Gb, say), play the song and then keep transposing around the circle of 5ths until you've played this song in all twelve keys.

5   Let's add a little soloing along with the melody. Now let's try playing just the roots in the original key and sing all of the 3rds. Now the 5ths. Now the 7ths. The 9ths. The 11ths. The 13ths. This is sometimes called singing the "functions" of the chords although I have no idea why. Don't assume this is easy, unless of course this is easy for you. If it isn't easy, do a little bit of it. If it is very difficult, play the 5ths and learn them as a kind of melody while you play the roots. Repeat this for as many of the functions as you can. Do as much as is interesting for you and as always, try hard not to beat yourself up about what you can and can't do, and just observe where the difficulties lie.

6   Now let's play the chords in both hands and sing an improvised melody. Don't try to find these lines at the piano, just sing them.

7   Now sing the roots and add notes around the roots. In this way, you can play bass for yourself as you solo over these bass notes. You don't have to be Bobby McFerrin for this one. Just use your knowledge of the roots of the tune to hold your place. You can miss a root here or there as long as you don't lose your place.

8   Repeat step 7, but this time visualize those notes on the piano (or playing them on your instrument if you are not a pianist) as you sing.

9   Okay, go back to the chords and singing. If you are a pianist, play the first four chords on the piano and sing a melody. Repeat that same melody, singing. (This will help you remember it.) Now find it at the piano or on your instrument. Do the next four chords, or just loop the first four for a while before moving on. If you are not a pianist, you can practice two ways: 1) play the roots of the chords

Tip #14 continued

been. A lot of that harmony comes from a background of knowing standards.

One last story and then we'll return to "Body and Soul." I had another gig with a group that was playing at the Knitting Factory (back in the day when more modern or "downtown" kinds of bands were playing what used to be called new music or avant garde jazz at the Knitting Factory), and the leader was a "new music" composer. His tunes had chord changes that were "new." They had a lot of triads and they moved in ways other than turnarounds. His desire was to be a "new" music writer, but what was new about the music? We were playing over vamps and chord changes. It was a lot like "old" music, but without the knowledge or depth. The changes felt stilted, unwieldy and clunky. I think it's important to go for the depth in the music, whether you are playing new music, bebop, Bulgarian music or three chord rock. Style isn't important—great playing is great playing. As someone who has played in both bebop-like situations and in free situations and likes to go back and forth between the two, I think there's a lot to learn in both worlds. Oops, one more last story. The first time I got to play in Tom Harrell's band, I remember the feeling of being on stage with Tom and Billy Hart. It was such a thrill. It was the first time that I got to play with Billy Hart, and his playing was so dramatic and energizing. We were playing all Tom's music, and at one point we were playing a tune that is essentially an extended blues. Soloing after Tom, I remember that feeling of trying to reach for something—for a depth in my jazz playing—to try to play up to Tom and Billy's level. The feeling I had from playing with them was that their ability to play jazz was deeper than mine and I had to try to match that depth, that swing, that knowledge of what makes jazz feel deep and profound. I have been pretty fortunate in that I've gotten to play with some incredible jazz players, and when as a younger musician I got to share the stage and

on your instrument and imagine a melody over it and then find it on your instrument; or 2) (the same as the pianist

method above) play the first four chords, sing a melody, repeat it and then pick up your horn and find the pitches, or find them at the piano.

10 Try to find the melody you are singing on the piano or on your instrument. If you make a mistake translating what you are singing to the piano, note the scale degree that you missed. (We've done this before, but it bears repeating.) Let's say you sang F Gb Bb C over the Eb-7 chord or 9, b3, 5, 6. When you played these notes on the piano you made a mistake on the last note, playing F Gb Bb Db. You mistook the b7 for the 6. So sing 9, b3, 5, 6 on all the changes of the tune. Sing b9 for dominants where it's appropriate. Sing natural 3 for majors and dominants. Sing b5 and b6 for diminished chords and half diminished chords. Then sing b7 to 6 on all of the changes of the tune. (Again, sing the appropriate 7ths and 6ths on major 7ths, diminished and half diminished chords.) Now go back to our original drill of singing, repeating and finding the notes. After you've been through a few of these drills of mistaken notes, you will find that your hearing has sharpened and that you are hearing more of the chord changes than you were when you started.

11 Eventually you can streamline the process described in step 10. Play the first chord. Imagine a line. Play that line. If you make a mistake repeat step 10.

12 You can also do this away from your instrument. Visualize the notes being played as you hear the sound of the line in your head.

Tip #14 continued

try to solo after Sonny Stitt, Carter Jefferson or Joe Lovano, I felt the depth that they brought to what they were doing and how this was something for me to aim for. Some of the depth that I am talking about is experiential and artistic. It's about commitment and feeling—a lot of things that aren't really the main focus of this book. Some of the depth comes from a deep understanding of things like melody, form and individual expression. And some of it just takes practice.

Practice tip #15
Practicing in all keys.

This is an interesting one for me. When I was younger I rarely practiced in all keys and I've talked to at least one great musician who said that he didn't see the point in practicing in all keys. Why practice rhythm changes in A when you are almost never going to play it in A on a gig, and you know that, whether you want to or not, you are probably going to play it about a million more times in Bb? Still, I've come to use practicing in all keys as a mainstay of my practicing.

On my side, of course, are Charlie Parker and Coltrane and almost every hard bop musician that I've heard talk about keys, but that's not a good enough reason to do it.

Here's why it helps: When you play the tune in all keys, something funny happens. Let's say I am playing a tune like "Anthropology" and I don't remember some aspect of the ornamentation. I play it in six or seven keys and it starts to come back to me. Hearing the intervals of the tune again and again, I start to see that there is an interval that I like, that I wasn't as aware of before I started taking the tune through the keys. Or I see that there is more than one musical choice, and I can play either. (Check out how Bird varied the melodies of his compositions in different recorded versions. It's another instance of someone having the underlying form—in this case the main aspects of the melody—internalized, and each performance becomes a

SOLOING WITH AN EAR FOCUS WRAP UP

1   Memorize the simplest version of the chord changes you can come up with, focusing on the main key areas.

2   At the piano: play the roots alone. Sing the melody. (If you are not a pianist, do this anyway, but also play the roots on your instrument, singing the melody in your head.)

3   At the piano: play the melody alone. Sing the roots. (If you are not a pianist, do this anyway, but also play the melody on your instrument singing the roots in your head.)

4   Play the roots of the song in all keys, transposing by ear (not intellectually).

5   At the piano: play the roots and melody together in all keys, transposing by ear.

6   At the piano: play roots, sing: 3rds, 5ths, 7ths, 9ths, 11ths, 13ths.

7   At the piano: play roots (or chords); sing improvised melodies over them.

8   Sing the roots, adding ornamentation (soloing around the roots).

9   Sing a melody. Repeat it. Now find it on your instrument.

10   If you make a mistake, analyze it and sing the missed scale degree over each chord change of the tune.

11   Repeat step 9 away from your instrument, visualizing the notes of the melodies you are singing being played on your instrument.

Review Everything We've Done

Remember that as you work on this new tune you are developing a list of things that is available in any practicing situation. For "Body and Soul," we explored working by ear, working on voicings and working on the melody, but you can work on all of the scale options that we discussed earlier. You can do the big scale exercise, the little scale exercise, arpeggios, bebop scales, guide tone lines and chromatic approach note patterns. **(CD EXAMPLE 11: "Body and Soul" bebop-like scales)**

I have students with whom I've explored countless practice options, who still wait to see me to figure out what they should practice next. These aren't my favorite students. They aren't developing practicing chops. They are developing passivity, but I'll wait to harp on you about that until later.
So let's take a moment to review all of the practicing rudiments we've been discussing. These are things that you can work on whenever you confront a new piece of music.

Tip #15 continued

variation on that form. I can't think of a reason why these tunes should be played the same time after time, unless you want to play them unison with someone; and even then, there is a wonderfully expressive thing that can happen when bebop heads are played with slightly different phrasing or ornaments in unison (as in Ornette's late 50s early 60s bands). A melody that I was uncertain of becomes a melody that I am fluent with, once it has been played in a lot of keys. We've already talked about how unfamiliar keys force you to use your ears, since you don't have muscle memory to fall back on.

Practice tip #16
Playing what you hear

Playing what you hear is an often repeated dictum of jazz. Like a lot of often repeated dictums, it has a lot going for it, but is also often misinterpreted, and like all rules it can be profitably broken. When I was com-

SCALES

1 Play scales out of time (ascending and descending) for each chord.

2 Play scales in time in 8th notes (start at a slow tempo).

3 Play the scales starting anywhere, continuing straight up your instrument (the big scale exercise).

4 Play the big scale exercise using different scales for each chord.

5 Play the big scale exercise in different rhythmic values (triplets, 16th notes, etc.).

6 Play all of the scales within the range of a 5th or 6th (the small scale exercise).

7 Play the small scale exercise varying scale options, rhythmic values and note order.

8 Repeat steps 1 through 7 using bebop scales.

ARPEGGIOS

1 Diatonic 7ths
   a Practice in 8th notes over the chord progression of the blues, starting on the first degree of the scale and moving up.
   b Start on any degree of the scale.
   c Displace an 8th note rhythmically (meaning, start on the "and" of one or the "and" of four).
   d Practice steps a, b and c in each inversion.
   e Compose a solo using diatonic 7hs as the primary ingredient.

2 The big chord (chord tones and scale tones together)
   a Practice playing the whole arpeggio for each chord change.
   b Try singing the arpeggio.
   c Break the arpeggio into four note units (1 3 5 7, 3 5 7 9, 5 7 9 11, 7 9 11 13), and practice each unit over all of the chords of the blues progression.
   d Practice steps a, b and c in each inversion.

3 Upper structure triads
   a Practice arpeggiating upper structure triads wherever the progression allows.
   b Practice the above step in all inversions.

4 Diatonic 4ths
   a Practice as diatonic 7ths above (only perfect 4ths).
   b Practice as diatonic 7ths above (perfect 4ths and combinations of 4ths and tritones).
   c Practice all inversions of b.

Tip #16 continued

ing up in the jazz scene in Cleveland in my 20s I was really into bebop. I was playing with the aforementioned bass player that had played a lot with Barry Harris, and he was trying to help me achieve a more laid-back feel—very important to the values of that group of players. (Playing with a laid-back rhythmic feel is important for a lot of different styles of music, but it is a particularly high priority of bebop players, and the bassist I was referring to could really play relaxed, making fast tempos feel slow.) Anyway, I said, what if I have a great time on a gig and I record it and my time sounds rushy when I listen back to it? Go with what you feel in the moment, said the bassist. He didn't mean that I should always rush, and taping myself is a valuable tool in terms of hearing what is going on in the band. But in the end when you play you shouldn't sound like you are being careful so as not to rush and if you feel good in the moment, then go ahead and rush. I think playing what you hear is something like this. Try to hear things at the piano. Sing to find out what is in your ear. Don't edit what you are singing. Finding it on your instrument is a good next step. Singing the chord tones and tensions for each chord encourages you to input those sounds into your ear. But when you are playing—go for it. I hate hearing people play carefully as if nothing is at stake and as if all the real improvising happened before they got to the gig. If you never make mistakes, perhaps you aren't pushing the envelope enough. Having said that, I think working on hearing more and more of what you are playing is one of the most important things to practice. When I listen to a solo of mine, I can tell the parts that I am more connected to. Often these are the parts that I hear most clearly.

One last thing on the "hearing everything you play" issue. Here's a quote that I've heard attributed to Sun Ra: "I don't want you to play what you hear, I want you to play what you've never heard before." I think that speaks to the importance of going for it, trying to go beyond

PLAY THE MELODY IN ALL KEYS

SOLO AROUND THE MELODY

VOICE THE MELODY

1 Left hand 1 and 7, right hand melody.

2 Add 3rds of the chords below melody in right hand.

3 Fill in chord tones and available tensions below melody in the right hand.

CHROMATIC APPROACH NOTES

1 Pick some simple patterns such as 1 2 3 5 or 1 3 5 7 and replace one or all of the notes with the 12 chromatic approach note patterns.

2 Make the roots of the chords the target note of the 12 chromatic approach note patterns.

3 Repeat step 2 with the 3rds of the chords, then the 5ths and 7ths.

GUIDE TONES

1 Compose several guide tone lines over the chord progression.

2 Improvise many guide tone lines over the chord progression.

3 Repeat step 2, singing.

4 Pick a line you like and memorize it.

5 Practice ornamenting that line, adding notes and melodic embellishment.

EAR-FOCUSED SOLOING

1 Memorize the simplest version of the chord changes you can come up with, focusing on the main key areas.

2 At the piano: play the roots alone. Sing the melody. (If you are not a pianist, do this anyway, but also play the roots singing the melody in your head.)

3 At the piano: play the roots alone. Sing the melody. (If you are not a pianist, do this anyway, but also play the roots singing the melody in your head.)

4 Play the roots of the song in all keys, transposing by ear (not intellectually), moving all of the roots a particular interval.

5 At the piano: play the melody and roots together in all keys transposing by ear.

6 At the piano: play roots, sing: 3rds, 5ths, 7ths, 9ths, 11ths, 13ths.

7 At the piano: play roots (or chords) sing improvised melodies over them.

8 Sing the roots adding ornamentation (soloing around the roots).

9 Sing a melody. Repeat it. Now find it on your instrument.

10 If you make a mistake, analyze it and sing the missed scale degree over each change of the tune.

11 Repeat step 9 away from your instrument, visualizing the notes of the melodies you are singing being played on your instrument.

But now we have to move on. Let's put our developing practice techniques into the service of learning a clearly hard tune, "Giant Steps."

CHAPTER 5: *"Giant Steps" – Changing Chords Really Fast*

"Giant Steps" is something that I use a lot when I work with students. On the one hand it is difficult but it offers a very clear problem that we can creatively apply ourselves to. The problem is switching chords (and chord scales) rapidly.

First, it's important to think of where "Giant Steps" comes from. In 1959 when Trane recorded "Giant Steps," he was interested in superimposing chords over cadences. He was already very adept at playing changes, and so he was investigating adding more and more changes for smaller periods of time to his chord progressions to create a blur of harmony—something like an aural mosaic—by moving quickly from one chord to another. The way Coltrane plays on each chord is very precise. His lines go through the heart of each chord change, which helps emphasize the rapidly shifting harmony.

Modern playing has moved in two seemingly opposite directions: 1) toward more changes in a smaller spaces of time, creating a kind of harmonic maze for the soloist, and 2) more open space and longer periods of time on one chord.

Trane had been exploring this second approach with Miles Davis during this period. 1959 was the same year that "Kind of Blue" was recorded. Actually, these two different approaches often turn out to be related. When playing over open forms, players can superimpose other harmonies over them. This is something that Trane had been doing and was to continue a few years later when he moved to more open one chord forms in his compositions, but for now on tunes like "Giant Steps," "Countdown," "Satellite" and "26-2," those complex changes were written into the song form.

Okay, so here is my own personal history with this song. I was playing every week at a club in New York called Augie's. Augie's was a dive, but a lot of great younger musicians played there. I had been playing there with a great trumpet player named Scott Wendholt for three or four years, and at this point I was working there regularly with an extremely talented tenor sax player named Joel Frahm. Joel is a great and extremely facile musician. (I remember when I was doing a clinic with Joel and he said that students should check out Charlie Parker and he launched into a Bird solo that he had listened to a lot years before. He played about four choruses, took the horn out of his mouth and said that he had started with Bird's solo but didn't remember all of it exactly. "I was paraphrasing," he said.) Anyway, he is that sort of player—a very good memory, great pitch and time and very quick-witted as a soloist. Anyway, Joel would play "Giant Steps" at a fast tempo every week **(CD Example 12: Joel Frahm playing Giant Steps)**, and every week I would play a less than stellar solo on it. After about six months of this weekly humbling, it occurred to me that I could practice this tune. Now, it took me a while to think of this, because I had never really cared much for "Giant Steps." It seemed kind of academic to me; the harmony followed a pattern and it seemed a little mechanical. I was more into the "open" thing—Miles with Herbie and Wayne, Ornette and Keith Jarrett and later Trane. I didn't really want to hem myself in with a lot of chords.

Anyway, I started practicing the song. I started with what I could do easily. It wasn't obvious what that was in this case. I mean, I'd been playing the tune every week, and I only knew it as something that was hard. I had to be willing to play the simplest things on it and to do no more than that until I had internalized each simple thing and could go on to the next, slightly less simple thing.

As I said before, it takes a lot of humility to practice well. I knew that I needed to start at the beginning and make a new start with this tune. I had to be willing to assume that I really didn't know anything about how to play on it. I think that sometimes our egos stand in the way of our progressing. I often meet with students who are trying to convince me that they know more than they do. That's fine. In this world, people who pretend to know a lot often convince the rest of us. But when you are by yourself in the practice room, then the ego has to disappear. You have to ask yourself what is truly easy to do—what is as close to effortless as you can make it. The next day when you start practicing the same tune, you have to ask yourself again, what is the easiest thing you can play on this tune. If you start where you finished the day before, assuming that you don't have to go back to the beginning again because you must have mastered whatever you started yesterday, then you are going to miss something.

Working on this tune was useful for a lot of reasons—the difficulty of spelling rapidly changing chords, finding ways to loosen up the harmonic rhythm, singing things and ear training and lots more—but maybe the most important thing it taught me was how to practice something hard. Here was something that was undeniably difficult, I could vouch for that, and if I made progress at playing it, then I would have found a method of studying that bore fruit.

So how do we practice this tune? I once gave a workshop on this topic at the request of several students and after the workshop one of the students came up to me and said, "Okay, you gave us a lot of methods for working on this but I had really hoped you'd give me some cool lines to play over this tune." It was kind of like saying, "Hey, I know you taught me to fish so I can feed myself for the rest of my life, but I'd actually just prefer you gave me a fish because I'm kind of hungry." Not to get bitter or anything, but really. (Along these lines at the same school I once had a student that I had been teaching for a couple of years come up after a master class and say, "I have been looking for that information for the last two years. Finally, someone gives me

Practice tip #17
Keep it simpler

I recently heard a story about the great guitarist Ben Monder. Ben is a wonderfully gifted musician who has an extremely complex sense of harmony. He writes long, involved, beautiful and complicated music in different meters, using a unique palette of difficult finger-breaking chords. Anyway, a friend of mine asked Ben what he had been practicing lately, and he said that he had noticed that when he played the C major scale at a medium slow tempo, the notes weren't quite as even as he wanted, so he had been working on that. I think that sums up the perfect approach to practicing.

The most productive things to practice are things that are simple, and yet there is a bit of tension, or a lack of complete ease there. Working on those sorts of things, things that are really central to playing music, things that you almost know, has a huge impact on your playing. I think a lot of people practice around the periphery of what they need to be working on instead of honing in on the center.

That's why I tend to practice simpler things today. I may still be working on difficult problems, but the part of these problems that I want to attack each day has to be something simple.

this thing that I've been looking for! Man, I'm really angry at you—why did you wait so long?") Anyway, I recount that for the purpose of saying that to work on this tune effectively, I had to give up any notion of cool lines and of starting at a complex or sophisticated level. I had to try to find where absolute zero effort was, meaning what I could play without bringing in all the stress that I already associated with this tune.

So where is zero? I started with the melody. Could I play the melody? The melody of "Giant Steps" is actually constructed pretty ingeniously. An arpeggiation down a GMaj7 up to the minor third. Up a half step to the 9 on the ii chord (A-7), down a step to the 5 on the V7 (D7), and then up a 4th to the D and another arpeggiation of a major 7th—this time Eb—and back up to the minor 3rd. Again, up a half step to the 9 on the ii chord (F-7), down a step to the 5 on the V7 (Bb7), and then up a 4th to the 5th on the I chord (EbMaj7). Again, up a half step to the 9 on the ii chord (A-7), down a step to the 5 on the V7 (D7), and then up a 4th to the 5th on the I chord (GMaj7). Again, up a half step to the 9 on the ii chord (C#-7), down a step to the 5 on the V7 (F#7), and then up a 4th to the 5th on the I chord (BMaj7). Again, up a half step to the 9 on the ii chord (F-7), down a step to the 5 on the V7 (Bb7), and then up a 4th to the 5th on the I chord (EbMaj7). Then a ii-V back to the top. Look at the chords for the first two bars, the "Giant Steps" innovation of traveling up a minor 3rd to connect 3 different keys. If we start with this progression, it isn't intuitively obvious that a major 7th of one of the chord centers of the tune is going to connect the chords horizontally. Also, speaking horizontally, the sound of a major 7th (7,5,3,1) followed by its minor 3rd is a very interesting sound and hints at an interesting color relationship between the major 3rd movement of the three key centers of the tune (B, G and Eb) and the minor third root movement of the dominant 7ths following major 7ths.

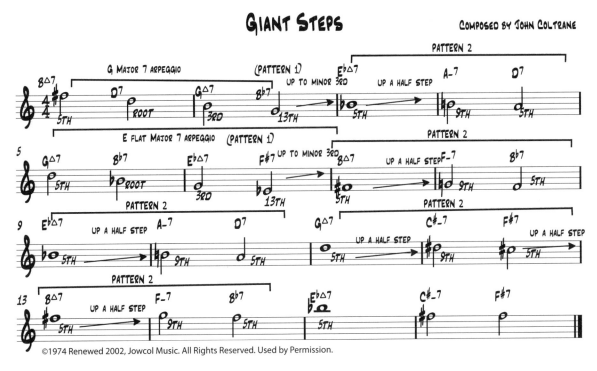

But I should be speaking more personally here. What could I play of the melody when I first started working on this song? Maybe if I played it with the roots in the left hand I would play the F#, D and B correctly, but then I would be unsure of the next note, I might get that wrong. I've heard students make that mistake many times. The G is the weird note because it's a 13th on the Bb7; all of the other notes are chord tones over the chord that they each occur on. Again, my ears might betray me there. But not if I limit my practice to the melody. So that's where I started.

Since I have been talking about what a great tune "Giant Steps" is to practice, let's practice it together.

100 rainy day activities to perform on "Giant Steps" (or "Giant Steps" in 100 tiny steps)

1 Play the melody of "Giant Steps." (Pianists, play it with both hands in octaves.) Memorize.

2 Play the roots of "Giant Steps." (Pianists, play the roots with both hands in octaves.) Memorize.

3 (Pianists and non-pianists) go to the piano. Play the roots in the left hand, sing the melody.

4 Play the melody in the right hand, sing the roots.

5 Let's do something different here. Play 1 and 7, 1 and 3, or 1 and 5 in the left hand. Play the melody in the right hand.

6 Fill in voicings for above. Try to make beautiful rich voicings using the natural tensions (no altered tensions for the most part) with the melody on top.

7 Let's look at the left hand. (The next few steps aren't so complex that non-pianists can't handle them.) Play 1 and 7 for all of the changes.

8 Play 1 and 7 for the major 7ths and ii-7's and and play 1 and 3 for the V7's.

9 Play 1 and 5 for all of the chords.

10 Play 3 and 7 or 7 and 3 for all of the chords.

11 Play these standard voicings: 3 5 7 9 for the ii-7 chords, 7 9 3 13 for the V7's and 3 5 7 9 for the major 7ths. Play also the inversions of these voicings—7 9 3 5 for the minor 7ths and major 7ths and 3 13 7 9 for the V7's. These are sometimes called A and B voicings.

Practice tip #18
Alterations on "Giant Steps"

The dominant 7th chords in Giant Steps usually take natural tensions, meaning natural 9 and 13 instead of b9 and b13. I alluded to this earlier, but I want to spell it out. The reason why I suggest you start by limiting the amount of alterations in your tensions, is because "Giant Steps" is about changing chord scales fast— three key centers juxtaposed every 2 beats or 4 beats. When you alter a dominant, you make it less like the key center that you are leading to (the I chord that the dominant resolves to) and more like the key center you just left. For example, b13 on the D7 is Bb, suggesting the harmony of either the B major key (7) or the Eb major key (5). Natural 13 is B, which suggests the harmony of either B major or G major, the key center you are moving toward. So by playing the b13 on the D7 you are obscuring the "G-ness" of the D7 (or its function as a V7 chord in G major). The quality of juxtaposing very clear but different colors in close proximity to each other is lessened—the colors become less clearly differentiated. Remember, you have very little time on each chord change, so you probably don't want to obscure your sense of the rapid modulations in this form. Also, playing through the changes clearly is the challenge of this tune. Having said that, this rule (like all rules) is made to be broken if you feel a creative urge to do otherwise.

12 Repeat steps 7 through 11 with the melody in your right hand.

13 Repeat steps 7 through 11 with the roots in your right hand.

14 Repeat steps 7 through 11 with these voicings in the right hand and the roots in the left.

15 *(For pianists and adventurous non-pianists) Let's get more interesting with voicings in the left hand. Let's try some non-root voicings that aren't these stock voicings. The 4-note common voicings that people play sometimes sound kind of blocky and dense—let's try some smaller voicings.

Here's another version with some similar voice leading ideas:

Using voicings that have 2 or 3 notes in them thins out the left hand and allows the left hand voice leading to be heard more clearly. It also gives the right hand melody or solo more space, since it isn't competing with a more dense left hand.

16 *(For pianists and adventurous non-pianists) Practice coming up with 2-note and 3-note voicings for the whole tune working in 4-bar units.

17 *(For pianists and adventurous non-pianists) Repeat steps 15 and 16 with the voicings in your right hand and roots in your left. (For non-pianists, repeat steps 5 to 17, arpeggiating the voicings on your instrument.)

18 Let's look at how we can create some material for the right hand. Try to construct 2-note voicings for each chord in a way that is similar to what we've been doing for the left hand. Use voice leading, and start with any intervals that you think might be interesting. Here's one possible example

Now you can try breaking the line into quarter notes, like this.

19 What we are practicing here is being able to choose interesting notes over rapidly changing chords. You should spend a long time on familiarizing yourself with the chord changes through repetitions of step 18. Try it at different tempos. First play the intervals as harmonic intervals and then as melodic. This should give you some ideas about making lines over these changes. Notice that the voice leading that you use in constructing the harmonic intervals leads to lines that have a connected directional quality, like in bar 4 above, G to B to G# to B. We can hear the voice leading in the line. This notion of creating a single line that implies two different voices is something that we will return to when we are talking more about multi-line playing.

20 Now let's try the same thing with 3-note voicings. Again, this should just serve as an example; you need to find the 3-note combinations that interest you.

Now we can make triplets out of the above chords.

Or we could make 8th notes of these broken chords, varying the rhythm of the three notes, sometimes making three 8th notes and a rest, sometimes repeating a tone to make a mostly 8th note line.

21 Okay, having branched out into a few new approaches, let's recap some other things that you can do on this song; first scales: big scale exercise in 8ths, quarters, half notes, various triplets.

22 The small scale exercise at various rhythmic values and using different "windows" played in different areas of the piano: 5ths sized, 6th sized, octaves.

23 Bebop scales, connected in a big scale.

24 Bebop-like scales, with a freer choice of half steps.

25 Guide tone lines in half notes; try improvising many of these.

26 Guide tone lines; try memorizing one or two and then add ornamentation.

27 Approach note patterns. Improvise some half note tone guide tone lines and then try adding chromatic approach note patterns to each.

28 Diatonic seventh arpeggios.

29 Upper structure triad arpeggios.

30 Let's do something more ears oriented. When we last visited the ears side of things, we were singing roots and playing the melody and vice versa. Let's start there.

    a)   Play the roots and sing 3rds.

    b)   Play the roots and sing 5ths.

    c)   Play the roots and sing 7ths.

    d)   Play the roots and sing 9ths.

    e)   Play the roots and sing 11ths.

    f)   Play the roots and sing 13ths.

31 Now don't play the roots. Can you sing triads for all of the chords?

32 Sing the roots and add chord tones or scales tones around these notes.

33 How about a simple line? Pick one of the scalar things that you were working on and try to sing that, imagining the notes as you sing them.

34 Repeat step 33, but don't sing. Just imagine the sound of the line.

35 Pick another thing you've practiced: left hand 2-note voicings. Improvise four bars of this. Settle on those voicings; put them in your right hand with roots in your left. Now sing the voicings from the bottom note up.

36 Sing two handed voicings for the melody (note by note, of course) from the bottom up to the melody note.

37 Play the chords for the first four bars of the song and sing any lines that you hear.

38 If that isn't easy, simplify by playing just the roots and singing lines.

39 Sing a line over the first 4 bars of the tune and repeat it so that you can sing it the same way repeatedly.

40 Find the notes of the line.

41 Repeat steps 39 and 40 for the whole tune in 4-bar units.

42 If that is difficult use 2-bar units.

Practice tip #19
Singing voicings

So often students are stumped as to what to practice. Again, to borrow an affirmation from Kenny Werner, it doesn't matter what you practice—all that matters is how you are practicing. This is how I understand that idea: everywhere in music there are potentially interesting things to study. What can't you do? Okay let's start there. When I am working with students I often suggest for them to do things that I have never done. That's because I am not really attempting to give you a complete program or course of study. How do I know what you need in order to become the improvising artist you want to be? Hopefully, you are engaged in a process of experimentation and discovery through which your musical goals are taking shape. That is a process that can continue for your entire life. (Someone once asked Duke Ellington what his favorite of his own compositions was. "The next one," he said.)

Okay, end of pep talk. When you don't know what to practice, try singing voicings. Invariably you are playing more than you can sing, so try arpeggiating your left hand voicings. Try arpeggiating your two handed voicings up to the melody note. Do it for as long as it is interesting.

Practice tip #20
Using all of your tools of comprehension

Playing an instrument is a complex, multifaceted experience. Sometimes it seems like I am talking a lot about theory. Some people might object that they feel that hearing is more important and they want to forget the theory. Sometimes it seems like I am focusing inordinately on things that aren't rhythmic, and again some people might object that after all, it ain't the notes you play, it's how you play them. I haven't said much about spirituality—and after all, playing music at its deepest level is a pretty

43 Whenever you make a mistake, note the scale degree you missed. Make the missed passage into a pattern, something like 2357 for example, and then sing over each chord in the progression. (I know I am repeating myself. Some things bear repeating. And I'm going a lot faster this time.)

44 When you are away from your instrument, try singing these lines. Visualize the piano keyboard as you sing.

45 *(For pianists) Okay, let's try another tack. By now, you should have the form fairly well internalized. Let's leave out the roots and try soloing over the form with the right hand alone. This is always pretty illustrative.

46 *(For pianists) What kind of lines do you hear when you play with only one hand? Try doubling the right hand with the left hand. Does that change the type of lines you play? Try playing lines with only the left hand. Does that change the type of lines that you are playing?

47 Compose a chorus of a solo line over the progression. Try to make it as interesting as you can. Learn to sing it, then to play it. Analyze your note choices. What can you learn from doing this? **(CD EXAMPLE 13: Solo on Giant Steps – composed)**

48 Listen to a lot of recordings of your favorite players playing on "Giant Steps," starting with Trane.

49 Pick a few ideas from other people's solos and try to transcribe and then analyze these ideas. Try to figure out what the soloist was thinking so that you can employ some of his strategies in your own soloing. This is more important than lifting the notes.

50 Another way to gain control of difficult chord changes is to try to differentiate between chord tones and non-chord tones. So, over the first 4 bars... actually, let's start with the second 4 bars this time. I keep referring to the first four bars, but of course I imagine that you are working on the whole form in pieces. Anyway, starting with the second four bars, play a chord tone on the first beat as a quarter note and nothing on the second beat. On the third beat play a chord tone for the Bb7 and nothing on the

Tip #20 continued

spiritual undertaking. Other people might object that all this intellectual talk just muddies up the water—music is about feeling and experience. To all of these people I would say, I agree with you. It's a little like the story of the three blind people in a room with an elephant. The first guy, feeling the side of the elephant, says, "Hey, this thing is really big and broad and kind of tough, like a wall." The second guy, who is holding on to one of the ears, says, "No it isn't. It's big and loose and flappy and kind of wrinkly, like a big wrinkly garbage bag." The third guy, who is holding on to the trunk, says, "No, it's more skinny and long and the end is wet and it's moving around like a snake." Of course the moral of this old chestnut of a story is that they are all describing the same thing, focusing on different attributes. It's the same with music. You need to try to become sensitive to how you like to learn. Try some of my suggestions, but use the concepts we are talking about to develop your own ways. Maybe for you, ears are the key and that is what you practice. In that case you can challenge yourself to use theoretical ideas to bring new information to your lines. (Give your ears some new material to work on.) Maybe for you it's all about time or feeling or spirit. But can you use your intellect then, to present new information to you? Or maybe you are a theory head. You know all of the licks and what scales they come from. Maybe then you need to concentrate more on rhythm, time, storytelling and developing your ears.

Practice tip #21
Visualizing the piano

The piano is a harmonic instrument, a rhythmic instrument, a singing lyrical instrument. It is also a visual instrument, and the pattern of black and white keys is easily conjured up in your mind if you've spent any serious amount of time looking at one. When I am working away from the piano, I sometimes play it in my head—picturing the keys. The shapes that these patterns

fourth beat. On beat 1 of bar 5 play a chord tone for EbMaj7 nothing on beat 2 and a chord tone on the F#7 on beat 3 and nothing on beat four. Do this for the whole form.

51 Okay, let's reverse this: play nothing on beat 1 and a chord tone on beat 2. Play that over the whole form.

52 Okay, now play a non-chord tone (otherwise known as a tension) on beat 1 and nothing on beat 2, a tension on beat 3 and nothing on beat 4, etc.

53 Now, play a chord tone on beat 1, a tension on beat 2, a chord tone on beat 3, a tension on beat 4, etc. Please notice that you have a lot of choices here. For example, the first 2 beats could be B C#, B E, B G#, D# C#, D# E, D# G#, F# C#, F# E, F#G#, A# C#, A# E or A# G#—any of the two beamed 8th notes below.

54 Now do the reverse, a tension on beat 1 and a chord tone on beat 2, etc.

55 Now let's try 8th notes. Play all of these variations: A chord tone, tension, chord tone, tension for each chord change.

56 A chord tone, chord tone, tension, tension for each chord change.

57 A tension, chord tone, chord tone, tension for each chord change.

58 A tension, tension, chord tone, chord tone for each chord change.

59 3 chord tones or tensions (you can specify all of the combinations if you wish for 4 more steps) and one chromatic approach note

60 2 scale tones and 2 chromatic approach notes.

Tip #21 continued

of black and white assume (a D triad is a triangle, for example, although most of the patterns aren't so easily captured in words) become another way of retrieving that sound. It's funny, personally, I rarely look at the keyboard when I play although I have talked to some great pianists who find it necessary to keep in visual contact with the instrument.

Practice tip #22
Roller blading

I was in the middle of my period of absorption with "Giant Steps" when I began my unfortunate involvement with roller blading. I really loved roller blading, but I was awful at it. I have the sense of balance of a drunken toddler in a windstorm. I would go roller blading every day and I would fall and hurt myself every day. You know, I actually thought I was pretty graceful at it, but even when I was at my peak form as a roller blader, cars would pull up along side of me and the driver would lean out the window and say, "Keep at it! You'll get it!" And who says New York isn't a friendly place?

I had a good friend who was into running and so we decided we would go out together for our daily exercise. He ran around the neighborhood and up on to the Brooklyn Bridge and I followed. Now, the pedestrian part of the Brooklyn Bridge is composed of slats, wooden slats. I don't mean to suggest that a more gifted roller blader couldn't have made short work of the bridge, but for me it was extremely challenging. I got about a third of the way across and then decided I should turn back, but it was too late. I fell and twisted the middle finger of my left hand pretty badly. Anyway, I had a rehearsal a few hours later and then a gig at the Village Vanguard (I was playing with the big band during this period) and by the end of the night my finger was the size of... hmmm....well it was about 3 times its regular size. Unfortunately, I was leaving for a month-long tour in Japan the following day. This is how big a roller blading fan I was—even

61 Here's another idea. One way to work on practicing chords is to practice the notes that aren't available, the wrong notes. Comp the left hand chord change and play the 5 notes that aren't part of the usual chord scale for this chord change. (Non-pianists can practice this over a Music Minus One record, a computer program like Band in a Box, or a sequenced version of the roots of each chord change.) For example, on the first chord change, the B Maj7, C natural, A natural, D natural, G natural and arguably F natural aren't available, so play four of these 5 notes as 8th notes. Do the same over each chord change, finding the unavailable notes. You'd be amazed how difficult this is for pianists— we are so programmed to play the scale that corresponds to the notes we are playing in the left hand. But forcing yourself to split your brain like this—one part being aware of and playing the changes to the tune, one part playing all the wrong notes—makes finding the right notes of the chords child's play.

This is pretty hard so make sure you do this slowly.

62 Another quality that makes "Giant Steps" challenging to play on is the confining nature of the harmonic rhythm. What I mean by that is that less experienced players tend to hammer the chords changing every 2 beats in a heavy inflexible way. We hear the rhythm of the melody for the whole duration of the tune: change change change change change...change change change change change change change...change change change...change change change...change change change...change change change...CHANGE CHANGE! After a number of choruses of this relentless drubbing—the rhythm section would have long ago lost interest—the song can seem like an uninspired obstacle course. But the constancy of the harmonic rhythm actually gives you an opportunity to play against it by varying the harmonic rhythm, leaving chords out and then catching up with the changes of the tune. First let's try it with the melody:

Tip #22 continued

after my most recent injury I took my roller blades with me. I remember the first morning in Osaka I was roller blading around (they weren't popular in Japan at the time, so I elicited a lot of stares, and probably a few muttered, "Keep at it! you'll get it!" in Japanese) and I was standing at a stop light, and the next thing I knew I was sprawled on the ground as usual. This time I had a large gash across my face just below my eye. Well, I finally saw the light. I put my roller blades away and haven't been on them since. But the point of this story (yes there is a point) is that for the next month I was playing almost entirely right handed. When I had some practice time, I started playing "Giant Steps," but only with my right hand. This wasn't difficult for me, I could easily keep the form. But what I noticed is that my lines were kind of suspect. I had been using my left hand to define the harmony, and the right hand lines were directionless and kind of nebulous.

When I proceeded slowly and sang along with my right hand, I realized that I was hearing lines that were a lot different than what I was playing. Or in other words, I wasn't using my ears much while I was playing. What I was hearing was more like what Coltrane played. His lines define the harmony extremely clearly and simply: triads in different inversions, 1235 patterns, 1, maj7, b7, 1 for dominants, 1357 etc. So, I started playing and singing lines more like that since that was what was in my ear. I wouldn't have been aware of that if I hadn't been unable to use my left hand. This, sadly, was the only long term positive effect of my roller blading career.

Practice tip #23
Don't play what everyone else plays

This is a value that has changed a lot over the years. Sometimes when I hear a proficient student, I hear a lot of material derived from other people's solos. Look, this is often a transitional step toward becoming a proficient and original player. I think becoming familiar with jazz vocabulary is a great aid to studying. And there isn't anything wrong with playing what someone

Of course, we don't entirely get a sense of how displacing the melody can throw things off when we are playing quarter notes in the left hand. It sounds more displaced if the left hand follows the right hand:

So we'll start working on displacement of the harmonic rhythm by playing a constant left hand against the displaced right hand melody. When you are confident of that, move on to:

63 Displacing the left hand and right hand together. (Practice with and without metronome.)

64 So far we have talked about displacement in relationship to the melody, and we've practiced it in two ways: over quarter note roots and over roots that move with the chord changes. Needless to say, you should run through the melody many many times, improvising where the displacement occurs until this feels natural to you. Now let's go back to your fully voiced version of the melody

Tip #23 continued

else played as an exercise. When you are transcribing, you want to become as near to that person as you can become.

Still, I think that older players placed more stress on developing your own sound. I remember Cleveland legend Bill Dearango, a guitar player who had played for years with Ben Webster in the late 40s, telling me that when he was coming up, players would get hounded for playing too much like a master that they revered. If the players on the gig thought you were imitating someone too much, they would tell you and give you a hard time about

(step 6: if you skipped that one you can go back and do it now, or even better do it again and come up with another version of these voicings) and try improvising the harmonic displacements using fully voiced chords.

65 Now let's try using displacement over the blowing form: First just try improvising based on the ideas we've been discussing. Here's an example that might be illustrative and get you going in this direction. **(CD EXAMPLE 14: Harmonic displacement on Giant Steps)**

66 How did the improvising go? What ways might you try to develop this idea in your playing?

67 Your ideas:

   1)_____

68 2)_____

69 3)_____

70 4)_____

71 Okay, enough of your ideas. Well, not really, but if I wrote a lot of numbers down with spaces for you to write your ideas for the next 100 pages or so, I think I'd lose a few of you.

72 So here are some of my ideas about how to start working on rhythmic displacement on "Giant Steps." First, for the pianists out there, let's try some left hand rhythms. Oops, we've stumbled on to another large area. Let's backtrack a little. Rhythmic accents in the left hand help propel the rhythm section and give a swingier feeling to the right hand line. Getting control of these accents allows you to contribute more forcefully to the rhythm of the band and makes you less of a drag to play with. For those of you who aren't pianists, this is an opportunity to think a little more like a rhythm section player. Horn players so often begin their solos with a level of complexity that limits the possibility of interacting with the rhythm section. Rhythm sections communicate, to some degree, on the level of half notes and dotted quarters, anticipations of an 8th note. So, for pianists, let's start with what some of you might have

Tip #23 continued

it. Bill used to play with Art Tatum, and I asked him if he knew what he was playing or if he ever tried to transcribe Art's playing and he said, no, he'd listen to Art and then try to play something like it, or something that fit with it. Also, I remember the great alto player Bob Mover telling me that when he first started playing in Mingus' band with tenor player George Adams, he made the mistake of imitating the "sheets of sound"-oriented way that George was playing one night, and after the gig, George (a big man) cornered him and said that if he ever tried to steal his...("harmonic material" was the word I think he used) again he'd beat him up.

So, what to do. Everyone is different. I was lucky enough to play with Sonny Stitt just before he died, and he played a lot of things that were traceable to Bird; however, he had his own voice.

Anyway, seeing as how everyone gets to have an opinion, here is mine: I can't always tell if you are playing someone else's lines, but usually I can. And what's the point of sounding like Herbie when I can go buy a Herbie record or see Herbie the next time he is in town? What usually happens is that the solo you are transcribing is a response to a specific playing situation by a brilliant musician. When you trot out some of the slick bits in your solo, the situation is different. A drummer friend of mine, describing a pianist that plays a lot of Herbie-derived material in his solos, said, "You get these great licks, but then they aren't always played in time and anyway, what happens in between the licks? There's a big difference between the material that he has lifted and what he plays when he is improvising."

Still, it's a hard thing for people to come to terms with. I have some very bad news for a lot of you jazz piano students: You will never be Herbie Hancock. And for you younger guys, you'll never be Brad Mehldau either. Nope, not Bud, Barry Harris, Keith or McCoy. Mullgrew Miller is already taken. The Kenny Kirkland slot is also filled. On the up side, as the song

been doing naturally. Let's go back to the smaller voicings that you were working on (way back in step 15, when we were both a lot younger). If you have forgotten these, take this opportunity to work out some voicings in this style and settle on one set for the tune. Another option is to use 3 and 7 or the A + B voicings 3 5 7 9 and 7 9 3 13.) Play the whole tune, soloing with the right hand over these left hand voicings with the left hand falling on the downbeats 1 and 3 of each measure when there are 2 chords in a bar, and on 1 in the measure when there is only one chord per bar. For non-pianists, I want you to play the same rhythms: half note, half note, whole note, varying the notes. Play guide tones that outline the chords, play roots, thirds, 5ths, etc. Find interesting ways to connect these chord changes using the long rhythms below.

73 Change the left hand rhythm to the "and" of 4 if there is one chord per bar and to the "and" of 4 and 3 if there are two chords per bar. (Non-pianists, play the same types of notes as above, in this rhythm.)

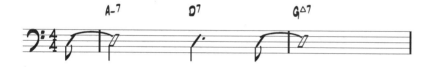

Practice soloing over this until you are comfortable. (If necessary, break this step down further—start with playing half notes in the right hand over this rhythm, then quarter notes, then eighths or combinations of eighths and rests.)

74 Change the left hand rhythm to the "and" of 4 if there is one chord per bar and to the "and" of 4 and the "and" of 2 if there are two chords per bar. Practice as above. (Non-pianists, play the same types of notes as above, in this rhythm.)

Tip #23 continued

says, there will never be another you, either. Sometimes it seems like this is the booby prize, but realizing the truth of this statement is an important step to becoming a creative practicer.

Having said all that, trying to see how other musicians think about chord changes is tremendously important. Just don't be too wedded to their notes. If possible, you want to be able to absorb things about the way they think, not re-create the notes of their solos when you are performing. More on the importance of transcription later, when we talk about rhythm.

Here are a few more words of wisdom from some giants:

"No one is original. Everyone is derivative." – Sonny Rollins

"Sometimes you have to play a long time to be able to play like yourself." – Miles Davis

"We all have idols. Play like anyone you care about but try to be yourself while you're doing so." – B. B. King

Practice tip #24
Displacing the harmonic rhythm

Not long after arriving in New York, I met and played a bit with the great trumpeter John McNeil. He was the first person to suggest to me that the line doesn't always have to change to the new chord at the downbeat of the new chord change. One can start thinking of the next chord a little early, or extend the last chord a little longer into the next bar. It wasn't until many years later that I started incorporating this simple and powerful idea into my playing. This is such an obvious thing to do and yet many students never think of doing it. This rigidity about switching chord scales at the point of the chord change can give your solo a kind of paint by the numbers quality, an inflexible sense of chord outlining instead of a dynamic breathing solo line. And, of course, the busier the harmonic rhythm of the song is, the more pronounced

75 Change the left hand rhythm to 1 if there is one chord per bar and 1 and the "and" of 2 if there are two chords per bar. Practice as above.

76 Change the left hand rhythm to the "and" of 1 if there is one chord per bar and the "and" of 1 and 3 if there are two chords per bar. Practice as above. (Non-pianists, play the same types of notes as above, in this rhythm.)

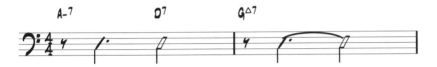

77 Change the left hand rhythm to the "and" of 1 if there is one chord per bar and the "and" of 1 and the "and" of 3 if there are two chords per bar. Practice as above. (Non-pianists, play the same types of notes as above, in this rhythm.)

78 *(For pianists) Now try playing only the left hand with the metronome. What accent patterns do you like? Has this increased your awareness of the upbeats that you can use for left hand comping?

79 *(For pianists) Repeat steps 73 through 77 with half-note roots in the left hand and the left hand voicing you were using in your right hand.

80 *(For pianists) Repeat steps 73 through 77 with the melody in the right hand.

81 Okay, let's return to the topic of harmonic displacement. Reorganizing the bar with these displacements is a little like creating many bars of mixed meter. For example, this harmonic displacement

Tip #24 continued

this quality becomes. I think this problem is an outgrowth of learning songs from lead sheets instead of by ear. On the page, the point of the chord change is fixed. The lead sheet says, change chords exactly here.

In the previously cited Marian McPartland interview with Bill Evans, Bill Evans dramatically illustrates his ability to make spontaneous changes in the harmonic rhythm of the tune. He cites this as one of the most significant developments in the evolution of his personal style and demonstrates on "All of You."

Anyone who is familiar with Bill Evans knows this quality of his playing. For example, in a standard ii-V-I progression (where the ii-7 is one bar, the V7 is one bar and the I chord is two bars) the ii chord and V chord might get 3 beats each, causing the I chord to come two beats early. Often he accents the harmonic displacement by reinforcing the new false downbeat with an accented voicing in his left hand. Bill Evans' style evolved toward greater harmonic precision in his right hand lines as well, often playing patterns and arpeggiations that clearly delineated the change in less beats, so that the displacement could be felt more strongly. By this I mean, if you are going to harmonically displace something, you have to be very clear in your statement of the harmony so that we can feel the rub of this harmony against the four square rhythm of the song. It's interesting to note that Bill Evans was often drawn to (and wrote or reharmonized so as to create) songs that had two beat chord changes ("How My Heart Sings," "Turn Out the Stars," "I Should Care," "How Deep is the Ocean," etc..) I would imagine that these songs with their busy harmonic rhythm afforded him the chance to push around the harmonic rhythm in a way that suited his playing.

Now that we are discussing altering the harmonic rhythm of a tune, the question always arises: what does the bass player do while you are changing things around? This question arises whenever we are talking about altering the harmony

could also be written like this:

Most people wouldn't write the above. If something can be written in 4/4, generally speaking, we write it in 4/4. But the meaning is the same for soloing; you get 3 beats on the first chord, BMaj7; 2 beats on the D7, GMaj7, Bb7 and EbMaj7; 3 beats on the A-7; and 2 on the D7. So, let's pick the following displacements to try:

BMaj7 (3 beats), D7 (2 beats), GMaj7 (2 beats), Bb7 (2 beats), EbMaj7 (3 beats), A-7 (2 beats), D7 (2 beats). (Practice soloing slowly over this form. Stop. Repeat. Gradually increase the tempo.)

82 GMa7 (2 beats), Bb7 (1 beat), EbMa7 (2 beats), F#7 (2 beats), BMaj7 (5 beats), F-7 (2 beats), Bb7 (2 beats). (Practice soloing slowly over this form. Stop. Repeat. Gradually increase the tempo.)

83 EbMaj7 (2), A-7 (3), D7 (2 beats), GMaj7 (5 beats). (Practice soloing slowly over this form. Stop. Repeat. Gradually increase the tempo.)

84 C#-7 (1), F#7 (3), BMaj7 (4). (Practice soloing slowly over this form. Stop. Repeat. Gradually increase the tempo.)

85 F-7 (3 beats), Bb7 (0 beats), EbMaj7 (4 beats), C#-7 (3 beats), F#7 (2 beats). (Practice soloing slowly over this form. Stop. Repeat. Gradually increase the tempo.)

Tip #24 continued

or harmonic rhythm of a song. The answer is always twofold: the bassist can go with the changes as he or she hears them or the bass player can lay down the changes at the normal time and the pianist will catch up with him eventually. Listen to Bill Evans and Eddie Gomez and you get a good example of this. People tend to notice how free Eddie Gomez plays and yet the thing that often strikes me is how he knows when it is important to provide a cadence point for what Bill is doing. Ultimately, the bass player is the one in the band who is most responsible for making downbeats. Nothing ever really sounds like a "1" (first beat of the measure) if the bassist doesn't play the 1. (This doesn't mean that the bassist needs to play on the 1 all of the time. What I mean is that when the band needs an anchor point, a clear definition of the downbeat at some point in the tune, that can't happen if the bassist doesn't play it. Think of a held V7 chord before the last I chord of a ballad. It's the bassist's job to define this ending and if the pianist and drummer hit it together and the bassist doesn't play, it sounds unresolved. The bassist makes ones.) Herbie Hancock, when asked who his favorite bassist was, replied that when he played with Ron Carter, everything felt anchored and he could play whatever he wanted. This anchoring function of the bass

...to page 93

86 Now put the whole thing together into a chorus. Break up the chorus as needed, and of course you can do the math and come up with some version of a harmonically displaced chorus of your own. The above displacements are just examples. This might be a good time to try to bring in the compositional approach and try writing a solo that incorporates many of the things we've been working on regarding displacements. Pick displacements you like, either mine or others, and try composing a line that conforms to those displacements of the harmony but is interesting as music. Learn this solo at various tempos.

87 Okay, enough about displacements. Here's another angle that we haven't explored that much—intervals. Let's try improvising a line of 8th notes that mostly uses 2nds:

It ends up being pretty similar to our scale approach. Well, that makes sense— scales are comprised of seconds for the most part.

Let's try improvising a line with 3rds. **(CD EXAMPLE 15: "Giant Steps" solo in 3rds)**

88 4ths: **(CD EXAMPLE 16: "Giant Steps" solo in 4ths)**

89 mixed 4ths and 5ths and tritones: **(CD EXAMPLE 17: "Giant Steps" solo in mixed 4ths, 5ths and tritones)**

90 Pick some other intervals that you think might make interesting shapes over these changes. Then compose a line mixing these ideas of interval focus and rhythmic displacement. Memorize the line and learn how to sing it.

91 Whew, the end is in sight. In these last few steps, let's focus on piano players, looking at a few piano textures that we haven't checked out yet. It might be interesting to try playing a stride left hand on "Giant Steps." A very simple stride left hand is comprised of a root on the first beat of the measure and a smaller higher voicing on the second beat of the measure. Let's use 3 and 7, although of course you are welcome to use anything that appeals to you. On the 3rd beat of the bar (if you don't have another chord change to play, play the 5th of the chord, if possible, below the root you played on beat 1. Beat 4 is 3 and 7 again.

Using these rules should have generated the left hand below, or something pretty similar. (Please note that I occasionally added a 3 and 6 voicing instead of the usual 3 and 7 for variety's sake on measures that have a major 7th chord for the whole bar..)

Practice this with melody in the right hand and with the melody in octaves.

92 Try playing this stride left hand with the melody in octaves with a 3rd inside the octave. That would generate this sort of right hand, an idiomatic sound with stride.

93 Try varying the interval, using intervals other than a 3rd to create a more colorful right hand.

94 Try staggering the rhythm of the right hand, playing an 8th note after the downbeat or anticipating the downbeat by an 8th note. If your left hand time is strong, these accents will push and pull against the beat and feel swingy.

95 Try soloing over the stride left hand. Start this way: play stride and sing over it, im-agining the type of lines that would complement this feel. Go slowly at first. Try loop-ing sections, using all of the tools that we have been working on in the last 94 steps.

96 Stride embellishment 1: adding to the "pah" chords. Essentially the stride pattern is "oom pah oom pah." (Refer back to step 91 if necessary.) The "pah" chords that we have been using are 3 and 7 (and occasionally 3 and 6. Notice that stride is actually a form of multi-voice playing—there is the line that the bass makes (sort of tuba-like, 1 5 1 5), another line that the top note of the voicing makes and a third line that the lower note in the voicing makes. If you play each line separately, or if you divide the "oom pah" up between your right and left hand you can hear this more clearly. Let's add notes to the "pahs," making 3 or 4 note voicings using the same sort of voice leading ideas that we used back in step 14. This will make it sound a little fuller, a little less bare.

97 Stride embellishment 2: adding to the "ooms" (1). There are a number of variations that you can try with bass function notes—the ones that come on 1 and 3. You can add to these notes, making them octaves or 10ths.

98 Stride embellishment 3: adding to the "ooms" (2). You can also change these notes by adding chromatic approach notes or passing diatonic chords before the next oom. This will eliminate a "pah," and can be a useful variation. Taking these last two steps, you might come up with something along these lines

Tip #24 continued

has something to do (at least rhythmically) with making downbeats.

In the example of displacing the melody against the quarter note roots of "Giant Steps," you can see that eventually things work out, even in an example where the bass is playing roots on every quarter note. In this example, you can measure the displacement against something. No one gets lost this way, although if you were playing with a bassist who was doing that, you might feel a little bit confined. But now we are getting to a whole universe of playing issues that are probably a bit beyond the scope of this book. The bass function of providing an anchor for the band is such a slippery and subtle one. Some bassists play almost entirely quarter notes and yet the time feels open and giving—you can play what you want, displace like crazy and it never feels locked in. Another bassist playing all quarter notes keeps you from displacing much and feels more confining. Some bassists seem to intuit what you are doing and some play in such a way as to cancel out every idea you have. Of course, the real issue is the composite rhythm between the soloist, bass and drums. Bassists (as well as everyone else in the band) have to focus on the groove and also respond to harmonic ideas as they come up. For young bassists this can feel like walking a tightrope. For old pianists working with young bassists, it can feel like walking a tightrope while carrying a young bassist on your shoulders, but I digress.

99 Another interesting embellishment that stride players use to great effect is turning the beat around. "Oom pah oom pah" can become "oom pah pah oom," "pah oom pah," "oom oom pah oom oom," etc. Some people think of this as groups of 2's and 3's and it is really quite similar to some of the things we were working on in the harmonic displacement section.

100 Other pianistic approaches. We are almost through with "Giant Steps" and it seems we've barely scratched the surface. Walking bass in the left hand would be a great thing to add here. To construct a simple quarter note walking bass line over this tune, write down the rootsof the chord changes on the 1st and 3rd beats whenever there is more than one chord per bar, and on 1 whenever there is only one chord per bar. Now add chromatic approach notes on beats 2 and 4 when there are 2 chords per bar, and just on 4 when there is only one chord per bar—you needn't follow the harmony here; an Ab leading to a GMa7 is permissibleon a D7 chord change. For the remaining missing quarter notes, try to move by step. These steps should generate a line similar to this one:

(I broke the rules just a bit here and there to make the line more interesting, and I encourage you to do the same.)

Well that's it. 100 things to do on "Giant Steps." If we kept going we could probably come up with 100 more. Here are just a few of the things that I didn't mention, some of which we will investigate in later chapters: playing lines doubled with two hands in octaves or at another interval; possible reharmonization choices; multi-line playing; transposing this song into other keys; playing the melody in the left hand with chords in the right hand; soloing with the left hand with right hand chordal accompaniment; soloing with the left hand underneath the melody—not to mention a world of rhythmic variations, including odd meter, mixed meter and different feels; using pentatonics in a variety of ways; playing different pedals under the different sections; reharmonizing with slash chords; and the list goes on.

What is the point of all of these ways of practicing "Giant Steps"? I guess that I have a few different goals for what I'd like you to get out of this. On the most basic level, perhaps some of the ways of working on this tune will help you address what you think might be weaknesses in your playing. That would be very good, and I'd be glad to be of help in that way. On a deeper level, I would like you to think about your thinking process. I'd like you to look at how we took this tune apart, working on different aspects in different ways, always looking for ways to get to find out more about this tune, but looking for easy incremental steps to cover the territory we are exploring—trying to find simple solutions to the difficulties of improvising over a complex structure.

In the kind of teaching I do, I often generate lists, as you have probably gathered by now. The reason that I generate lists is because there are a lot of ways to work on becoming a better improviser. Sometimes when confronted by one of these lists, students' eyes glaze and they say something like, "Holy Moly, Berkman" (Robin was a student of mine), "that's a lot of things to do! I'll never get through all of those things." With respect, this is the wrong attitude to have about lists of things to do. You're right, you'll never get through all of those things. So pick one and see if it leads you someplace interesting. All of the lists are really just methods of getting to something that you are interested in. Once you are there, the lists don't matter anymore. You're doing it. You're practicing.

Tip #25 continued

or her playing. I don't know that I practiced this in a very specific way when I first started playing that way. Sometimes just hearing someone play something suddenly makes something clear that you didn't understand before. I had an epiphany listening to the Herbie Hancock trio once that I'll share with you later (and no it wasn't that I would never be Herbie Hancock, I didn't have that epiphany until many many years later). Anyway, along the way in your practice when you start working on some element, you should always try to freely improvise with it and see if there are things that are intuitively clear to you that you don't need to develop through practice. The reason I haven't mentioned this before is because, based on the students I have had, not practicing comes pretty naturally. But the kind of not practicing that every teacher sees in his less enthusiastic students is not really what I am talking about.

Practice tip #26
The difference between not practicing and what I am talking about

I'm going to paraphrase Dick Oatts again. Students practice with this idea—they are trying to take something outside of themselves and bring it inside, into their playing. They need to practice more with this idea: trying to bring something that is inside of themselves out. What I mean is, you have to stay engaged. You have to improvise and see what sounds you like. You have to think about whether you like what sounds you are making. I don't mean this in the sense that you need to edit out the things you don't like. I mean this in the sense that you should be looking for the next interesting thing that will engage you. It's part of that task of becoming the singular player that you are. So I am assuming that you are playing all the time, searching for what is going to grab your attention next, listening a lot and being moved by all of the amazing things that people play. In that context sometimes a simple

Tip #26 continued

idea is enough to change things in your playing.

Here's another quote that almost fits here:

"If ya ain't got it in ya, ya can't blow it out."
– Louis Armstrong

Practice tip #27
The limitations of jazz education

Of course, that's the goal—for you to be able to do this yourself. And there are some students who really respond to this—the "fill it in yourself approach." I was doing a master class at the school in Holland where I teach regularly, and I asked for questions and a student asked, "Why do you talk so much? I think we just need to play more and get our asses kicked." And of course he was right to an extent—after all, that is a lot of how I learned. The point of a lot of these stories that I keep regaling you with is that there are a lot of experiences that you have to have to develop as a musician. Hopefully there is a place for both talking and ass kicking. This reminds me of another story: I was doing a workshop with the great drummer Tom Rainey and a group of students were playing a blues for us. At the start of the bass solo, the drummer's volume was too loud, but he didn't notice for a while because he was trying to signal to the rest of the band members that after the bass solo, he wanted to trade 8's. After the tune ended, Tom lit into the drummer for not listening to the other band members. "I'm trying to think of a reason why a bass player would ever call you for a gig," Tom said. "No wait, let me change that...I am trying to think of a reason why ANY-ONE would ever call you for a gig...." Tempers flared, but a point was made. When it was my turn to talk we worked on

playing at different volumes, listening to different instruments, etc. Things cooled down. We bonded. After the workshop, Tom and I talked about the experience. He said that he didn't see the point in spoon feeding the music to students. He didn't learn that way and he didn't know anyone who had. His point was that students have to want to go out and get it—to try to figure out how it's supposed to sound. They have to work actively to get good, not wait for someone to tell them how to do it. I agree to a large extent, although I usually employ a somewhat less confrontational style and have been guilty from time to time of a little spoon feeding.

One of the most often repeated observations that jazz musicians make about jazz students is that a lot of them seem awfully passive. (In a way, telling a teacher that you don't want to absorb any more talking and want your ass kicked is the ultimate passivity. Go out and kick your own ass! Although, that does require a flexibility that is beyond most of us.) Students can download 60 GBs of music, but then how well do they know a single solo, like Herbie's solo on "Autumn Leaves" or Lennie Tristano's solo on "Line Up." Similarly, on a recent google search I found lots of free transcriptions of Keith Jarrett, Sonny Rollins, Charlie Parker and every famous jazz musician you can name, but it's a different experience if you live with the solo and transcribe a single chorus yourself. A lot of students have a disc with 15 real books on it, but I'll go to a student jam session and find that the only tune everyone knows from memory is "Blue Bossa." Of course, these are extreme generalizations—only you know if they apply to you. Let me just say that there are a phenomenal amount of resources avail-

able to studying jazz that weren't available 20 years ago, but, at the risk of sounding like the curmudgeon that I am, I am not certain that the music has grown according-ly. Yet jazz education is a fact of life—the music has moved into the schools in a way that I wouldn't have predicted 25 years ago when I was living in Cleveland and working around town in small clubs with older, more experienced players. A lot of those playing situations no longer exist, and jazz education has grown to fill this void. Still, it is up to the individual student to buck this trend toward passivity and take an active hand in going out and getting the music, not waiting for it to come to you.

Practice tip #28
Listening for piano textures

In our whirlwind tour through stride and walking bass techniques as applied to "Giant Steps," I set out some of the standard techniques and variations. Of course, whole books can be (and have no doubt been) written on all the different things you can do with stride. What is set out here is just intended to get you started. The best thing you can do to augment your sense of what it should sound like is, of course, to listen. Great stride players can be found in a wide variety of styles and eras, from James P. Johnson and Jelly Roll Morton to Willie the Lion Smith, Fats Waller, Count Basie, Duke Ellington, Andrew Hill, Jackie Byard, Thelonious Monk, Hank Jones, Cedar Walton, McCoy Tyner, Oscar Peterson, Jimmy Rowles and Keith Jarrett. Each of these pianists has adapted stride to his own ends, to make a personal musical statement.

The same thing could be said of walking bass playing for piano, especially if we were to include organists in

this group. Pianists that have made use of walking bass in their solo playing include Tete Montoliu, Hampton Hawes, Dave McKenna, Lennie Tristano, Oscar Peterson and of course many others. Sometimes the line between piano styles is arbitrary. A lot of pianists (Tommy Flanagan, Oscar Peterson, Hank Jones for example) combine these styles into a solo piano style that is rich and varied.

Even if you never play stride on a gig, you will get a lot from working on it at home. For one thing, it might suggest a more active left hand. Another possibility is that it will make the chord changes audible to you in a way that you hadn't experienced before—there is something beneficial about the completeness of stride which so thoroughly spells out the harmony of the progression with bass notes (alternating the 5th of the chord with the root) and 7 and 3. Both of these styles are good for developing your time feel, because you are responsible for every quarter note. They are both solo piano styles that emphasize the completeness of the piano in laying out a groove and as such are extremely helpful in working on your time and groove.

I came to working on stride on "Giant Steps" after trying a lot of other approaches. I don't know that I have used it much in performance, but I really felt that it solidified certain things in the harmony of the tune that I hadn't felt as solid before I started working on it. I found that when I soloed over the stride left hand at a slow tempo, my lines were different from the lines I had been playing on the tune before, and that is of course the goal, to effect a change or open up some new territory for exploration.

CHAPTER 6: *Rhythm Changes, A Slippery Form*

Hmmmph. Rhythm changes after "Giant Steps"? That's a crazy way to organize a book on jazz. Everyone knows that rhythm changes come first and "Giant Steps" comes second. "Moten Swing," "My Little Seude Shoes," "My Little Brown Jug," "I Got Rhythm," "Anthropology": old; "Giant Steps": new, or newer at any rate.

There is a certain logic to that, of course. "Giant Steps" is a more modern response to traditional cadences, an experiment in superimposing chords over ii-V-I, or a way of using 3 keys to get to a major7 chord instead of a ii-7, V7 to get to that same major 7. But in some ways playing on rhythm changes is a lot harder than playing on "Giant Steps." I don't just mean in the sense that a lot has already been said on rhythm changes, or that "Giant Steps" has a complex harmonic structure that gives you a lot of suggestions about what notes you should be using at any time. (Meaning, when you play a hard tune with a lot of chords in it, your choices are more limited, so in a way it is easier to play on.)

Rhythm changes are hard for students because they have trouble figuring out which changes to play. Rhythm changes, like blues and the more simple standards, are harder to define because when people play on them they are constantly varying the changes as the solo dictates. When even strong mature players play on "Giant Steps," most of the time they are soloing over the standard changes of that song. Look at Trane's solo for example. He nails the changes. But when players play on rhythm changes, even traditional players, they use a lot of variations in the changes they are playing chorus to chorus. Consequently, rhythm changes as a form is more slippery than "Giant Steps."

So what is the deep structure of rhythm changes? Here things get easier, because on the deeper level of structure, rhythm changes is pretty simple. The first four bars are turnarounds, so the structure is really I in the first and third bars and V7 for all or the second part of bars 2 and 4. Bar 5 is a dominant or a ii-V leading to IV on the downbeat of bar 6. The second half of bar 6 is either a IV7 of IV, a IV-7, or a #iv diminished. Bar 7 and 8 are a turnaround and the first ending. The second ending is a ii-V in bar 7 and I in bar 8. The bridge is a series of extended dominants starting on the III7, each lasting for two bars. (So VI7, II7 and V7 or for those theory heads out there, more correctly: V7/V7/V7/V to V7/V7/V to V7/V to V7.) The last A is the same as the second A section. The problem, of course, is that this deep structure can be interpreted in so many ways.

The First Four Bars

So here are some of the choices for the first four bars of rhythm changes. (Note: the diagonal line pointing to the I chord in the first bar are possible substitutes for the first 2 bars or the first 4 bars, meaning 4 bars of Bb7sus4 or Bbdiminished, etc.)

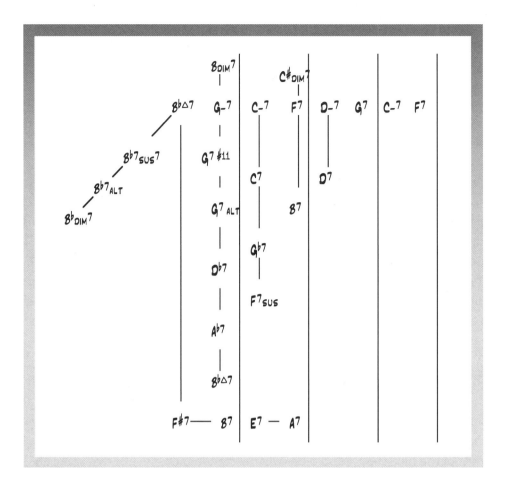

The chart above gives you some idea of the common substitutes for the first four bars of rhythm changes. The second 2 bars have all the substitutes available that the first two bars have, so I didn't bother to list them again.

Keep in mind that the deep structure for these 4 bars could be described as

or even as:

When we are examining rhythm changes, there are really two approaches to working on it. The first approach is the reharmonization approach, by which I mean, you can select all of the specific chordal options that you have, becoming fluent at playing and hearing these different options so that you can vary them freely. The second approach involves taking off from the underlying basic structure and seeing how you can reharmonize more freely, deviating from that structure as well as superimposing other harmony over it. It is a little like the two approaches in modern playing that we discussed earlier in relation to "Giant Steps," one approach being to fill in the form with a lot of chord changes, and the other approach being to vary freely over a more simplified chordal framework (as in modal jazz).

Let's start with the first approach. Working on all of the various substitutions available to you on this song is a little like working on "Giant Steps"—if we had about 20 different choices for the first 8 bars. Let's focus on the most common ones:

1 BbMaj7 G-7 | C-7 F7 | D-7 G7 | C-7 F7 |

This is the simplest way through the chord changes. It can be almost entirely diatonic to Bb if you choose modes of Bb major for the above chord scales (excepting the G7 in bar 3), or you might want to use more colorful scales on the dominant chords, perhaps altered or diminished on the G7 and F7.

2 a. BbMaj7 G7 | C-7 F7 | D-7 G7 | C-7 F7 |
    b. BbMaj7 G7 | C7 F7 | D-7 G7 | C7 F7 |
    c. BbMaj7 G7 | C7 F7 | D7 G7 | C7 F7 |

These three variations are common variants that are somewhat less diatonic than the first set of changes. The minor7s in each case are replaced by dominant chords, and these function as secondary dominants. The C7 might get Lydian b7 but the other dominant chords usually get diminished or altered. In any case, you have some latitude and would do well to check out all of the dominant scale possibilities for these chords.

3 a. BbMaj7 Bdim7 | C-7 C#dim7 | D-7 G7 | C-7 F7 |
    b. BbMaj7 Bdim7 | C-7 C#dim7 | D-7 Db-7 | C-7 B7 |

These two variations use passing diminished chords. They are also extremely common. Note that the Bdiminished in the first bar would be similar to playing a G13b9 there (same scale). The C#diminished in the third bar, on the other hand, is a different sounding choice from any F7, the chord that often appears in that spot. (It is a very different scale choice.) This chord is more like a V of D-7 (A13b9).

4 BbMaj7 (or Bb7) Ab7 | Gb7 F7 | Bb7 Ab7 | Gb7 F7

This is the variation of rhythm changes that works with the composition "C.T.A." by Jimmy Heath. (It may predate this tune, but that's how I know it.) It's become part of the substitute options on rhythm and people who don't know the song "C.T.A." often know this substitution. Again these dominants are usually not very altered, for a similar reason to the dominants in the "Giant Steps" progression, to increase the sense of momentary modulation down a whole step, and so take either Mixolydian or Lydian b7 scales.

5 a. BbMaj7 Db7 | Gb7 B7 | D-7 Db7 | C-7 B7 |
     b. BbMaj7 G7 | Gb7 F7 | D-7 Db7 | Gb7 B7 |
     c. BbMaj7 Db7 | C7 B7 | D7 Db7 | C7 B7 |
     d. BbMaj7 G7 | C7 B7 | Ab7 G7 | C7 F7 |

These and other variations utilize tritone substitutes for the dominant chords above. Like the above variations, these dominants use Mixolydian or Lydian b7 scales. "Bemsha Swing" (Monk) uses this sort of substitution.

6 F#7 B7 | E7 A7 | D7 G7 | C7 F7 |

This variation is a series of extended dominants that lead to the V7 chord in the 4th bar. For a good example of this check out the Sonny Stitt/Sonny Rollins trading on "Eternal Triangle" on Dizzy Gillespie's Sunny Side Up recording. It is a more extreme example of reharmonization than the previous variations and so is dependent on the rhythm section catching this as it goes by.

7 BbMaj7 Bb/D | Eb Edim7 | Bb/F G7 | C-7 F7 |

The first two bars of this variation also work for bars 5 and 6 of the A sections. It is more common as a blues turnaround but also can be found in more triad or 6th chord oriented rhythm changes like "Funjy Mama," "St. Thomas" (not exactly rhythm changes but has a similarly repeated turnaround section of the tune) and "My Little Brown Jug."

All of the above variations should be practiced just as we practiced "Giant Steps" using techniques such as the big scale, small scale, bebop scales, singing over roots, LH voicings, 3-note voicings, guide tone lines, chromatic approach note patterns, diatonic 7ths, upper structure triads, diatonic 4ths, 5ths and intervals of your choosing, harmonic displacement, "wrong notes," alternating chord tone and tensions and everything else.

The Second Four bars

The next 4 bars are a ii-7 V7 to the IV chord, then iii-7 VI7 ii-7 V7 for the first ending and ii-7 V7 I for the second ending.

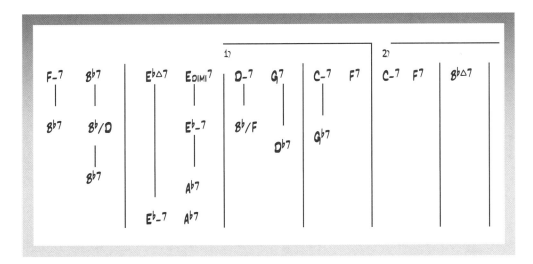

There are fewer options for the second 4 bars than the first 4. Here are some of the main options

1 F-7 Bb7 I EbMaj7 Edim7 I D-7 G7 I C-7 F7 I

2 Bb7 Bb/D I EbMaj7 Edim7 I Bb/F G7 I C-7 F7 I

3 Bb7 I EbMaj7 Eb-7 I D-7 G7 I C-7 F7 I

4 F-7 Bb7 I Eb-7 Ab7 I D-7 G7 I C-7 F7 I

5 F-7 Bb7 I EbMaj7 Ab7 I D-7 G7 I C-7 F7 I

Of course, you can come up with other combinations of these substitutions. Also you can substitute dominants for any minor 7ths and you can replace any dominants above with tritone substitutes as we did with the first 4 bars. Once again, you should practice the above using all of the techniques derived from our study of "Giant Steps," listed previously.

The Bridge

The bridge has a very different harmonic structure. It starts on the III dominant and then goes up in 4ths 3 times to get to the V7 of I. Common alterations include the tritone substitutions and the addition of related ii chords.

D7		G7		C7		F7	
A-7	D7	D-7	G7	G-7	C7	C-7	F7
D7		Db7		C7		B7	
A-7	D7	Ab-7	Db7	G-7	C7	F#-7	B7
Ab7		G7		Gb7		F7	
Eb-7	Ab7	D-7	G7	Db-7	Gb7	C-7	F7
Ab7		Db7		Gb7		B7	
Eb-7	Ab7	Ab-7	Db7	Db-7	Gb7	F#-7	B7
D7	Ab7	G7	Db7	C7	Gb7	F7	B7

In addition to working on all of these variations, the versions of the changes that have one chord for two bars give you the opportunity to try more than one chord scale over these dominants. Dominants often go from Mixolydian to a more altered sound like the b9 diminished scale or the altered scale. (Essentially, this would be the same thing as playing Dorian over the ii-7 of a ii-7-V7 followed by the altered scale on the V7. This is also the same as playing the Mixolydian scale on the D7 for the first chord change followed by the Mixolydian on the Ab7 change in the next bar. Look over tritone substitutes in the Theory section of this book if you are feeling a little fuzzy about these details.) This is a very important sound on dominant 7ths. The sound is of the natural tensions (Mixolydian) moving to the altered tensions (b9, #9, b13). This is very useful when you are working on voicings that have moving inner lines in them.

One other variation not listed above is also fairly common—it comes from Bird:

D7 Eb7 I D7 Ab7 I G7 Ab7 I G7 Db7……etc.

This is a variation that is superimposed over the chord changes—the bass player doesn't have to catch the up-and-down-a-half-step movement of this particular version of the chords with you. Because these chords are all interrelated, there is a fair amount of freedom between what you are playing and what the bassist is playing. You can easily be a tritone apart and it still sounds consonant for the reasons listed above. Moving up and down a half step is a simple reharmonization tool that you can use whenever you want because of the clear resolution. (When we were talking about the bass line on "Giant Steps," we saw that bass lines are usually constructed with a lot of chromaticism, especially in the beats that come right before the point of a chord change, and that is a device that you can use when you are comping or soloing.)

As I said earlier, there are two ways of thinking about this harmony: one is as a set of chord changes that exist together, nested in each other like Russian dolls. Working on rhythm changes in this fashion involves learning the 20 or so most common variations and then being able to call up one or another depending on what you are hearing. Here's an example of what I mean by this approach to playing. **(CD EXAMPLE 18: Rhythm changes soloing using various common substitutions)**

The other way of thinking about the changes of the tune is more fluid and maybe a little subtler. This method is more about learning the deep structure of the song and improvising sounds over that structure, not settling on any particular set of chord changes as the "right" ones for the form. (Of course, there is tremendous overlap between these two methods—learning all of the variations allows you to be freer with the chord changes of the tune, but there is also a subtle difference between playing "rhythm changes variation number 8" at the top of the chorus and just keeping the structure of the tune in mind and playing whatever form you need in the moment to develop your solo.)

The Deep Structure

So let's return to the deep structure of this tune:

Practice tip #29
Name that chord

Along these lines, I used to play with a trumpet player who always played on one of these 4 different variations for the first four bars of the blues (in F):

1 (regular) F7 | Bb7 | F7 | C-7 F7 |

2 (chromatic) F7 | Gb7 | F7 | B7 |

3 (Bird) FMa7 | E-7b5 A7 | D-7 Db7 | C-7 F7 |

4 (Dance of the Infidels changes by Bud Powell) FMa7 | F-7 Bb7 | A-7 G-7 | F#-7 B7 |

and as a comper, it was my job to hear which set of changes he was using and to comp the right one. I know that this was my job, because if I played the wrong set of changes the trumpet player would complain to me. We would also get together to practice outside of the gig and he would drill me on it. This is a way of playing (and comping) that I tend to associate with older players—players who all know the same vocabulary of common reharmonizations and expect the other musicians on the bandstand to hear "their" changes as they play. As an extreme op-

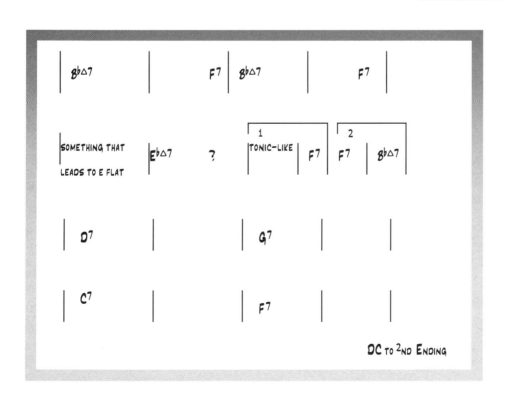

I remember a great article that Richie Beirach wrote for his column in *Keyboard Magazine* in which he tried to explain that, as he developed his solo over a blues, the chord progression became simpler and simpler for him. He found that later in the solo he used a more basic blues form (or played more directly on the simpler, deeper structure of the form, we could say) but played more complicated chromatic material over that form.

That's one of the important ideas about this deep structure concept—it is freeing because you aren't focusing on the details. When I try to find the deep structure of rhythm changes I am attempting to answer this question: What is the least amount of harmony I can give you, and still be clearly playing over the form of rhythm changes? Whatever that is will be the deep structure of the song. I can always add chords and chordal variations whenever I want if things feel like they are getting too abstract, so the deep structure doesn't cancel out any of the previous versions of the chord changes—it just gives us a way of thinking about what is most important and what we can change without throwing the people we are playing with too far off.

The deep structure doesn't have to be exactly the same for everyone. By this I mean that the deep structure for one person on rhythm changes might have F-7 to Bb7 in bar 5 (ii-V to the IV chord in bar 6) but for another, that bar is open as long as there is a cadence point at bar 6 in Eb (IV). For someone else the deep structure might require turnarounds for the first 4 bars, whereas another person thinks of that as a Bb-ish area. Because all of these sounds are interrelated, all of these players should be able to play well together if they are listening.

I remember getting to play with Sonny Stitt in a house band for four nights in Cleveland when I was pretty young and inexperienced. He called a few tunes that I knew as modal tunes (I remember one was "Softly as in a Morning Sunrise") but when I listened to him solo, I realized that he was thinking of these chords as minor turnarounds (C-7, A-7b5, D-7b5 G7b9b13), and so I comped accordingly.

Some of this way of thinking about the deep structure of tunes is conducive to a more modern way of playing, but the same sort of thing goes on in "straight-ahead" solos. I am thinking of the passage in Sonny Stitt's solo on "Eternal Triangle" that I

Tip #29 continued

posite approach, I used to play with the aforementioned Bill Dearango who always asked me to comp the harmonic substance without playing the harmony of the tune. This piece of zen-like comping wisdom is worth pondering. Another way of saying this might be, try to comp some of the harmonic movement of a particular set of changes without spelling out completely what you are doing. Small chords as opposed to 10-note two-handed monster chords can be an aid in doing this, but I digress.

Practice tip #30
The Herbie epiphany

At this point in the book, some of you must be feeling pretty nostalgic for all of those practice tips. I know I am. But we started talking about rhythm changes and the life just got sucked out of everything. (This sometimes happens with rhythm changes.) Anyway, now that we are talking about deep structure I want to share the Herbie Hancock epiphany that I talked about earlier with you. I was listening to Herbie Hancock play trio with Buster Williams and Al Foster. I would guess this would have been in the mid to late nineties. Anyway, he was playing on "Just One of Those Things" and that was a tune I knew. He was just tearing it up in a ridiculous mind boggling way and he got to the bridge. It was one of those moments where the tension was building and he played a phrase and then took it up a half step and then took it up another half step and then another. I was ecstatic listening to him and then it hit me. I know the bridge of this tune and the chords don't go up in half steps. In F, (although I think he played it in Eb, but usually it's played in F) the bridge starts on Eb then turns around and then ii-V's to C. It was somewhere in this part of the tune that he started going up in half steps. Anyway, I had always assumed that when players "took it outside" a little they were just substituting some other set of chords for the harmony of the tune. Listening

alluded to earlier, where he plays a Bb diminished scale (whole half or natural 9 diminished scale) for the first 3 bars of the form over the turnarounds that the band is playing. I always wondered what he was thinking about there. I mean, you could say that he's turned the whole first 4 bars into a kind of C13 b9 that leads to the F-7 in bar 5, or you could say that the Bb diminished sound is bluesy against the I major, or that it is a kind of color chord variation of I major (IdimMaj7), but actually, I don't know what Sonny Stitt was thinking. He plays this different color that has the effect of opening up the sound of the harmony for a moment and then slides right back into the harmony.

This sort of thing can be found in all sorts of straight-ahead solos over rhythm changes: the harmony opens up with a BbMaj7 for two bars, or a Bbdiminished sound, or the blues scale, or a chord that is a half step up and then the soloist brings back the V7 or plays on a secondary dominant that leads to a ii-V and we are back in the 2 beat changes for a while, until the next moment when the soloist opens up the harmony again. Below is an A section from Sonny Rollins' solo on "Eternal Triangle" that treats the first four bars of the A section as a Bb7:

This sort of playing is an extreme example of something jazz players do all the time. I have had a number of classical musicians study jazz improvising with me and this is always one of the really difficult things for them to do because it's a skill that they never use playing classical music. The skill that I am talking about is monitoring the progress of a form being played in time, while you ignore parts of it, substitute things,

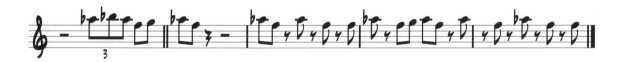

One way that soloists can do this is by thinking of common tones. Remember common tones? We haven't talked much about them in 80 pages or so, but when we looked at them last, I suggested that they would obscure the differences between the chords and that it might be a good idea to de-emphasize them for a while in your playing to create that sense

change the feeling or superimpose harmonic elements or cross rhythms over that form. Even when you are playing completely straight-ahead bebop-influenced music, you are using this skill constantly. You are feeling the changes go by, and you are playing a melody over those

of defining harmony precisely—the change spelling that we were talking about. Sometimes the opposite thing is needed: if you are stuck playing arpeggiations of chords for every two beats on a complicated form, common tones can help you create a feeling of elongated space—a more horizontal feeling of longer harmony. Take Sonny Rollins' melody, "Oleo." This is a beautiful example of common tone relationships, using only the notes of the Bb scale (with the exception of a chromatic leading tone to the 3rd on the F7 at the end of the 4th bar) to create a line over the A sections of rhythm changes.

Tip #30 continued

changes, cadencing in slightly different places, substituting a tritone, leaving a chord change out to thin out the texture and making a million other decisions. Your attention has to be in two places at once, feeling the structure go by in the background and improvising in the foreground. Classical musicians never ever have to do this. (They do some amazing things, but this is something that doesn't apply to them.)

Work on creating long melodies with a lot of common tones by playing through the form slowly, playing guide tone lines that are constructed entirely of notes from the Bb scale. You will have to be careful about avoiding notes that don't work over particular chord changes, for example if you are playing a B diminished on the third beat of the second measure, you can play Bb, D, F, and G, but not C, Eb, B or A. I would alternate playing common-tone-focused guide tone lines with the opposite, guide tone lines that are focused on the notes that change chord to chord.

So they have a tendency to get lost when they solo over chord changes. If you have a tendency to get lost, then you need to find out what is the most you can do and still be able to keep one eye on the form. What are the things that you are trying to do that take so much of your attention, that you can't do them and still keep your place?

Anyway, so that was my epiphany—that Herbie was doing something fundamentally different from reharmonizing as I understood it. I had understood reharmonizing to mean choosing from one of several known-beforehand sets of chord changes, picking something logical, a set of chord changes. Maybe there was a certain amount of spontaneous invention in it, of course, but the rules were probably fairly com-

COMMON TONES

So, how do you open up your playing by thinking about the form in a deep structure way? Here's an example:

I start with an idea, a whole step and 4th over Bb. I develop that idea, playing a 4th and a whole step, still on the Bb pentatonic, the left hand also contains the same intervals, my linear idea is based around an interest in 4ths and whole steps and I am going to use 4ths and whole steps comping as well. Why 4ths? Well, that is the sound I am going for, but part of the attraction is that they are less harmonically spelled out, a little more ambiguous, so they help create the sort of openness harmonically that I want. The line that opens the second bar is also on the Bb pentatonic and features the 4th prominently. Note that this one happens on the beat, the first bar starts off the beat on the "and" of one. Okay, so far so good—I am pretty firmly in the key of Bb, although I have chosen voicings and notes that stress the common tone qualities of the changes to help create a certain amount of harmonic ambiguity. The second half of the 2nd bar goes up a half step to C#7 sus (B pentatonic), and I have taken the notes of the first half of the bar and transposed them up a half step. It's important, I think, to have a strong motivic connection in your lines as you move away from the changes, because you are trying to create a logic to what you are doing—why are you playing these notes? Again I think back to the story about Herbie cited above: the line wants to go outside of the harmony and you are following it. At the beginning of the third bar I go up another half step, which changes the sound of our harmony—we aren't playing pentatonically here because pentatonic scales don't have

Tip #30 continued

prehendible. People who play more complex harmonically probably just know more complex rules, I would have thought. But here I was hearing Herbie do something different from that: he was freely changing the form, in fact leaving the form for a time, but without ever losing his place in the form so that he could return to it at any moment. It's a little like watching a train going into a tunnel from a distance. You might not see it for a few seconds, but if you keep moving your eyes at the same rate tracking what its progress must be, then you will be right with it when it emerges. So as you track the form, you can play things that aren't right, that are off, as long as you keep your sense of where you are and find a musical way to connect your outside idea back to the form again when you meet it further down the road.

Often re-connecting to the form means finding an important cadence point, perhaps the beginning of a chorus or some other significant landing place in the harmony somewhere. If you hit that, then everyone knows where you are and it's clear that your visit to a land beyond the form was intentional. If you get lost

half steps, but I am using those sorts of intervals: whole steps, 4ths and minor 3rds, breaking up this F# Dorian scale in that way. In the 4th bar we go back up to the A; again the half step is a significant sound because it contrasts with all of those major 2nds. The major 3rd that leads to the F natural is also a significant change because it is another new interval and it moves us back to the normal changes of the form, but I chose those notes thinking intervallically. We needed another sound to contrast with all of that F# pentatonic-ish stuff. In bar 5 we are back on track—note that I continue with 4ths in the left hand and some of the same interval shapes over the Bb7 and G7 altered, with whole steps over the C-7 in bar 8 and with linear material that moves up a half step in the second half of the bar.

The above example shows my thinking process in moving away from the changes. Mostly, I am thinking about intervallic relationships and motivic continuity. I also chose to move up a half step, and the harmony that I am using here has a lot of common tone relationships with the normal harmony of the tune. What I mean by that is, playing F#-7 is a lot like playing the altered scale in F, so I haven't really gone too far from the changes. That's partially because if I want to start on the changes and return to the changes in 8 bars, I am not going to stray too far. Also, I think this kind of close sideslipping sort of playing is easy to conceptualize. The same sort of thing happens in more extended freer passages.

Let's go for something a little more extreme. I might try to take a sound that is clearly NOT Bb and introduce it into my line. How about GMaj7? That's pretty un-Bb like and not very F altered either. Or is it? Over F we could think of it as natural 9, #11, 13 and b9, notes that don't exactly suggest a particular F chord scale but still are comprehensible as a kind of F chord. Or as a Bb with 13, b9, 3 and b13. How about C Maj7? This chord has the benefit of having the natural 9 and b9 in Bb, and over F is a major7. So let's try and use both of these:

in what you are playing and lose the form, then it might sound wrong or accidental. After all, not playing the changes isn't much of an accomplishment in and of itself, any novice can do that. Not playing the changes intentionally, meaning choosing some harmony that creates friction or dissonance, and then resolving at some point and continuing playing on the changes, is something that requires control and a keen sense of the form. Sometimes I tell students that playing the chord changes is what you do when you don't have a better idea. Which is simply another way of saying: in the end there aren't any rules that you can't break. Sometimes I want to hear the other notes, the "unavailable tensions." Sometimes I play the chord that doesn't fit because I am craving something dissonant, or just different. A lot of these sounds don't really sound dissonant to me—they sound like they are borrowed from somewhere else. They have a feeling of bitonality and sometimes they are kind of tense. Some musicians are happy with less tense sounds on chords and don't feel the need for these tones.

At a gig recently, a tenor player told me he was surprised by the amount of tension I was able to keep going in a solo. I think it was intended as a compliment, but I'm not really sure. In either case, if this is a sound that interests you, it's something that you can start looking for. I would say that this is another of those qualities that define modern playing, a desire to push the envelope a little further before the resolution.

Of course, if I were really developing these ideas in a soloing situation, I would spend a lot longer on these unusual changes. The above example feels a little forced to me. When you play these "wrong" chords quickly, they don't register on the ear enough and I want to really feel the rub against the regular harmony. Again, the important thing is the intentionality of what you are doing. You want this dissonance to register as something that you clearly intended, not as a lack of harmonic knowledge or inability to play over the chord changes. You can even use this idea when you are playing in a more traditional setting: if you make a mistake and play the wrong note, play it again and it will sound like you meant to do it. Of course, this isn't a panacea. Wrong notes sometimes just sound wrong, but intentionality has a lot to do with whether a note sounds good or not.

Sometimes I'll pick four of the "wrongest" notes on an F blues, notes like E natural, Db, Gb, and A and have students improvise over the form with only these sounds. This exercise shows what you can do with rhythm, motivic ideas, space and feel. Also, as we adjust to the sound of these notes we get used to the dissonance and find ways of using these "wrong" sounds for the unusual colors they have.

I want to emphasize something that I said earlier: playing more freely with the harmony isn't entirely stylistic. By that I mean, you can open up the harmony in less tense ways that are appropriate for bands that aren't especially modern, where the playing in the two previous examples would be out of place.

Here are two quick examples of that:

The previous example uses a Bb diminished scale in the manner of Sonny Stitt on the "Eternal Triangle" alluded to earlier.

This above example uses a Bb-11 in a similar way. Notice that the part that follows the more open section is influenced harmonically by the previous line.

Of course, I can open up the second 4 bars instead of the first 4. Here's a fairly outside example held together by whole step movement of motives and harmony. I am starting at the top of the form and the example lasts for 2 A sections.

That one is fairly extreme, but demonstrates a couple of useful ways of thinking about playing outside that I have been trying to emphasize. For one thing, when I go outside there is usually some relationship to the ideas that came before it. For another, once I start going outside, I might develop the idea through several keys, one of which might have a connection to the place where I am eventually planning on cadencing. Sometimes a new note at the point of the chord change acts as a kind of pivot for a new harmony (as in bar 12 above). I am not particularly conscious of most of this as I play, but often there is a certain logic to these harmonic moves, and that logic is derived from my split attention to both the changes that I happen to be playing and my sense of their relationship to the deeper structure of the song. Here are a few choruses of Bb rhythm changes at a moderate tempo that utilizes some of these techniques in a more organic, less academic sort of way. **(CD EXAMPLES19-21: 3 short rhythm changes solos that open up the form a little with more variation in the harmonic structure of the song)**

With that excursion into the outer reaches of rhythm changes, let's leave the universe of rhythm changes for now. These principles of opening up the form are something that can be utilized on any tune. Hopefully this quick look at the slippery world of rhythm changes will give you ideas of areas that you'd like to practice in your own way. Before we finish with this entirely, I just wanted to list a few examples that you'd do well to listen to in trying to learn how to deal better with this form:

"Eternal Triangle" from Dizzy Gillespie: *Sonny Side Up* (Sonny Rollins, Sonny Stitt solo and then trade)

"Rhythm-a-ning" from *Thelonious in Action* with Johnny Griffin, Charlie Parker, "Moose the Mooch," "Steeplechase," "Anthropology"

Dexter Gordon, *"Second Balcony Jump"*
"Straight Ahead" from *Una Mas,* Kenny Dorham (with Joe Henderson)

"Oleo," Miles Davis (with Horace Silver and Sonny Rollins on Prestige, originally issued as "Bags' Groove," with John Coltrane *(Relaxing)* and Herbie, Wayne, Ron and Tony *(Live at the Plugged Nickel)*

"Cottontail," Herbie Hancock

"Oleo," Herbie Hancock with Branford Marsalis

"Oleo," from *Don't Explain,* Joel Frahm and Brad Mehldau duo

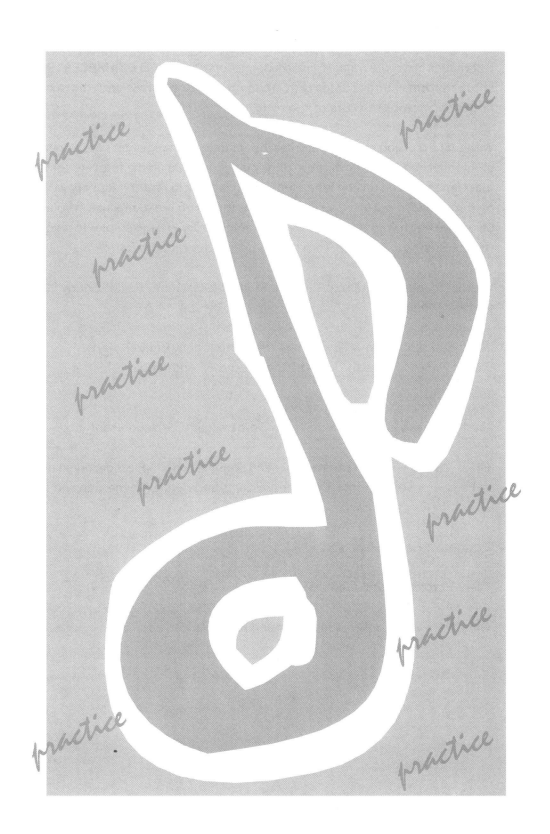

112

CHAPTER 7: *Rhythm, Deep Groove, Metronomes and Odd Meter*

Working on Rhythm

There's a terrific book about piano technique called *The Fundamentals of Piano Playing,* by Abby Whiteside, a legendary New York area classical piano teacher, and she opens her chapter about rhythm by saying: "Now is the time to believe in magic." That's because rhythm as a practice tool has an incredible effect. It allows you to organize your technique. It creates graceful playing. You can use rhythmic approaches to help you increase your understanding of the harmony of a tune. You can use it to help your ears. You don't really know anything musically until you can play it in time. Being able to play something complex at a slow tempo is usually a key step in integrating the new complex material into your playing. If you are struggling with a passage, try playing it in different rhythmic values varying between duple and triple meter. Rhythmic accents can help you develop fluency.

"And I just practiced on it and practiced on it. I found a lot of little things about details, about accents and how much of an accent to make."   – Herbie Hancock

In jazz, rhythm is perhaps the most important element of all. It's not what you play, it's how you play it. Everyone in the band is a drummer, in that we should all be able to groove and convey the time forcefully to the rest of the band and not be dependent on the rhythm section to make the music groove.

There is another quality that is magical about rhythm, and that is that people don't really understand very well how to practice it. It's slippery. It's subtle. It's about a feel. Students (sometimes) know when it feels good and (sometimes) know when it feels bad, but they are often unable to figure out why it feels good or bad and how to practice to make it feel better. It's a little like Supreme Court justice Potter Stewart's famous remark about pornography, when he declined to define it further saying, "I know it when I see it."

Well, that's not really good enough. (Not being a constitutional scholar, I'll leave it to others to decide if that's a good enough yardstick for pornography, but we have to take our study of rhythm to another level of sophistication. As for the study of pornography, you are on your own there, although a yardstick might still be a useful thing to have in that endeavor.)

So, rhythm. My formative experiences coming up as a young jazz player in Cleveland were often about rhythm. Nowadays I often coach young musicians at colleges, and that atmosphere is very supportive, very safe, but when I was in my late teens and early 20's playing gigs with older more experienced players, the mood on the bandstand could get pretty ugly over rhythmic differences. I used to work with an older horn player who would turn around exasperatedly in the middle of a tune and say, "just swing for Christ sake." For inexperienced players, it's useful to understand that older players may well get frustrated with you. They get frustrated because music matters to them and you are messing it up and getting in the way of their doing something they really love. Some fights on the bandstand come from people who care a lot about music wondering if you care that same amount. And if you care so much, how come your time doesn't feel good?

In many ways, I feel lucky to have learned in this environment. It taught me to value even more highly players like Wynton Kelly, Sonny Clark and Horace Silver, and later Kenny Barron and Mulgrew Miller, pianists who knew how to make a rhythm section feel good. I certainly appreciated these players before anyone yelled at me on the bandstand, but having someone tell me that I was a drag to play with made me check out these good-feeling comping role models with renewed interest. I learned to play smaller voicings in a more rhythmic manner and I learned how to leave space for other people in the band. I learned to play with a harmonic vocabulary that fit the musicians I was working with and play in the style of the band better. Older players schooled me about my rhythmic feel and taught me how to practice with a metronome.

The Metronome

Once I asked a new student if he owned a metronome and he said, "No, I don't need one. I have good time." While I have occasionally met someone with absolutely flawless time (something like perfect pitch, people who can play perfectly metronomically with seemingly no effort), they are rare and this student wasn't one of them. But more important than that was the attitude revealed about metronome practice. It's as if the metronome is there to bust you on your time. That's not what it's for, at least that isn't the only thing that it's for.

I already mentioned Bill Dearango, the Cleveland guitarist that played with Ben Webster in the forties. He was truly an eccentric guy. He played on 52nd street in the late forties but later returned to Cleveland (my home town), opened a music store and got into electric Miles Davis in the seventies and

Practice tip #31

Listening like a critic versus listening like someone who is about to sit in on the next tune

I know a lot of critics and in fact some of them are my friends. (Some of my best friends are critics....well, come to think of it, not my BEST friends...) They are often people who care passionately about music, and for the most part they aren't making much money writing about it. But they are often at odds with players, and here's why: A critic can afford to have opinions about who is interesting, who is advancing the music and who isn't, what is really great and what is only mediocre. Players have opinions too, of course, but players' opinions are informed by an appreciation of how difficult it is to play music, how all of the great players are providing a lesson in how to play, how to comp, how to make a rhythm section sound good, how to have a sound and a voice—how, even on an off night, hearing Kenny Barron or Cedar Walton is a lesson in how to play jazz. I had an interesting experience that shed some light on this issue. I went to hear a band of a friend of mine at the Village Vanguard. Mulgrew Miller was in the band along with some other well-known musicians. I listened to the first set and was a little bored. They sounded good, but the music didn't really hit me. It felt a little like things I'd heard before, not really special. On the break, the leader came over and asked me if I wanted to sit in. I said sure, and he said he would call me up at the end of the next set. I listened to the second set with completely different ears, everything Mulgrew played was suddenly intensely compelling. I noticed how hip his voicings were, how swinging his comping was, how groovy and centered his playing was in general and how he helped direct the rhythm section and set up soloists. The soloists all sounded different too. On the modal burner, they really tore it up with fiery exciting

eighties. Anyway, his playing was an odd amalgam of swing and free music. He had an amazing right hand and a great, very percussive, rhythmic articulation.

Anyway, Bill was a metronome freak. He loved the metronome. He had a little Taktell mini, which was a burgundy colored little wind-up metronome. It was the kind with a stick and a movable slide that had a metal thing on it that was sort of triangular with two screws or bolts or something on it that looked a little like a face. (To be perfectly honest, it was a trapezoid, but I thought that might sound a little pedantic.) "Look at him," I remember Bill saying, "I can play whatever I want along with him and he just shakes his head back and forth and grooves." Here Bill rocked his head in rhythm back and forth. "It's like he's saying whatever I play—that's cool, man."

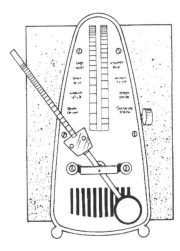

Playing with the metronome for Bill was never about getting busted. It was about grooving with this very groovy unflappable drummer. One time he was over at my house and he had me play a few notes over and over with the metronome (an old square box, a Franz I think, with the little blinking orange light on top) and he would just say, "No...no...that's not it—no...there...THERE...do you hear that? How groovy that was? Boy, when you get it, it's like night and day. When you play the time really groovy into the metronome, the beat gets really soft..."

Did I know what he was talking about? Sometimes I felt it, sometimes I didn't. But what I learned from him was that there was another relationship that I needed to develop with the metronome. I have friends that don't use the metronome and some of them have great time. Some people say that the

Tip #31 continued

solos. The point, of course, is that the band played similarly both sets but when I listened to the second set, I was listening with the ears of someone who was about to step in and play with them. All of a sudden, I became more aware of all the things that the group was doing, all the ways they were playing strong and rhythmically over the forms that they were working with, the subtleties that had eluded me earlier. I was listening to all of the things that I would want to do as a player in that same setting, some of which I could do and some of which I couldn't. For the first set, I was listening in a more detached manner, a little more like a critic. For the second set I was listening to what was there, not what wasn't there. That's why musicians almost always find critics too dismissive of master musicians, especially seasoned mainstream players, and a little overly taken with novelty. Critics also often tend to value whatever is current more than things from five or ten years ago, although of course this varies from critic to critic. Sometimes critics are new to jazz, having migrated from covering rock or pop music, and so they just don't have much familiarity with jazz history. Sometimes critics only like one style of music. Often in reviews, critics are telling you whether or not they like the music. Personally, I have no interest in whether a critic likes something or not—some people like chocolate and some like vanilla. Some people only like free jazz and some people only like hard bop. In any case, my point here isn't to trash or celebrate critics, my point is that you would benefit from trying to stop listening like one. Try and hear what is there and if it feels a little boring to you, try and listen at a deeper level to what the players are doing. There's a saying, the only things that are boring are things I haven't checked out on a deep level. (A friend of mine, a great alto player named Dave Pietro, always gives this advice at clinics: "Try to listen to a piece of music and not decide whether or not you like it." That's difficult to do. For many people, deciding whether or not they like a piece of music is the first

metronome is mechanical, and I think it IS important to shut it off and practice without it. I've seen some students get a little dependent on it, and obviously that is not a good thing. But, for me, the metronome is an invaluable learning tool. It gives me a guide to working on rhythms, it allows me to experience the front side of the beat and the back side of the beat. Mingus said there are 3 places to play on the beat, the front the back and the middle and he only worked with musicians who were sensitive to and could find all three places. I know that the practicing that I've done with a metronome has greatly improved my ability to find these 3 parts of the beat.

Incidentally, Bill was even more eccentric to play with than to hang out with. He would assemble the most dysfunctional bands imaginable. One of his beliefs was that jazz musicians didn't have good time anymore (too stretchy and hemiola oriented—no pulse) and that the guys with good time were playing funk. So sometimes when I played with him he would hire a funk bass player who knew no standards and any number of chaotic and unwieldy drummers who he might tell to play only brushes all night. (The only drummer he really liked that I recall playing with was Joe Lovano, who would sometimes sit in on drums if he was back in town. Often he'd start tunes we didn't know, certainly the bass player didn't know them, and he'd tell the bassist to just pedal an E. I remember a unique rendition of "Round Midnight" where Bill played in Bb-, I played in Eb- and the bassist played an E pedal. On that same gig, the bassist asked Bill if he knew Stanley Clarke's tune "School Days." Bill said sure and started playing the old nursery rhyme ("School days, school days, dear old golden rule days...") over a funk bass vamp. Sometimes he would just sit there, his walrus mustache framing a maniacal smile, while the guts of his guitar (an old thunderbird) were trailing out onto the floor. He was also the master of putdowns. Of one local pianist he said: "If he got an extension to his life of another 300 years, he still wouldn't have time to play a single note of jazz." Of a guitarist that had bad curvature of the spine, "He plays like he walks."

But there was a certain method to Bill's madness. He was fixated on the time—the rhythmic dimension of jazz. And he could deliver, in the right context. I remember hearing him play duo with a great mrindangam player, Ramnad Ragvan, who taught at the local university. Their rhythm was really

Tip #31 continued

thing they think of when they hear a new piece.) Often younger players have strong ideas about who they like and who they don't. I still have favorite players, some of whom you've been hearing about for the course of this book, but I am more appreciative of more players now than when I was younger. A lot of them are just too good not to like, even if you don't want to sound like them yourself.

amazing, like something physical in the room. On the few available recordings that I've heard of Bill playing back in the late 40s/early 50s you can hear a bit of this. Anyway, he was a big influence for me at a time when I was extremely clueless about rhythm.

I was fortunate to know and work with so many great older musicians in Cleveland at this time: Willie Smith, Lamar Gaines,Val Kent, Jacktown, Ace Carter, Greg Bandy, Jamey Haddad and many many others. The lesson from working with these musicians was all about time and groove. Whenever I would book a gig, I would always try to get one of these older players in the band, especially in the rhythm section if possible. My friends and I always felt if you had two young guys in the rhythm section it wouldn't sound good. When I teach now and hear bands of all young players, players whose main playing experience comes from playing with their peers, I am even more sure of the value of working with older, more seasoned players.

Okay, reminiscences aside, metronome stories aside, how do we start thinking about practicing time? (I have to admit, before we leave this subject altogether, I have an inordinate fondness for metronomes. I don't collect them or anything, but the old boxy wooden ones had a pleasant chock, chock sort of sound that the new ones don't have. I am not in the least bit nostalgic for the pyramid shaped stick ones, because they always developed a slight accent to the left or right and so weren't accurate enough. I had a Zenon quartz that I was partial to for about 25 years that only broke a few months ago. I'm making do with a Dr. Beat 66 these days—it has some nice odd meter possibilities, but it isn't the prettiest sound, although it's starting to grow on me. Some of the digital ones are truly atrocious sounding. Now, I really am sounding like Bill Dearango. That was another one of his quirks that I had forgotten until now. He was fond of everything that was in the past. He'd say things like, "Back years ago, things were cleaner. The air was better. Soft things were softer. Water was wetter. The color blue was bluer.")

Dave Leibman did a clinic recently at a school where I teach, and I was fortunate to be able to attend it. He advocates working on time through learning solos, first sung and then played with recordings. He teaches a course at the Manhattan School of Music where his students do just that. In Leibman's

Practice tip #32
Struggle

I want to go back to something I mentioned briefly just now. That time spent with Bill (and later alone) trying to analyze my rhythm and feel if I was grooving with the metronome was really important, even if the answer wasn't always apparent to me at the time I was doing it. Very often, dwelling for a while in the ambiguity of something you don't fully understand is good for you. Just mulling something over is good for you, even if you don't get the answer right away. Students have trouble with this concept. They are so used to immediate gratification. Students sometimes will complain that they can't transcribe something—that they aren't certain what a particular left hand voicing is, for example. If you listen to that voicing 100 times and you still aren't sure, but have investigated everything you think it might be, you have learned a lot even though the results aren't obvious. More often though, if you've listened to that voicing 100 times, you have a pretty good idea what it is. More importantly, if you've listened to it 50 times and still aren't sure, you've still been practicing effectively and will improve if you continue in this way. In practicing, the process really is more important than the result.

A friend of mine brought me to hear an older alto player that used to play on the street in downtown Brooklyn. (I wish I knew his name, because he was really great. He had a day job and didn't play gigs much, I think, although he knew a lot of the hard bop players from the late 70s or so in New York.) He played mostly bebop tunes and when he double timed he had that feeling that Charlie Parker had, not the notes exactly, but that amazing snaky feeling. I asked him if he could play "Confirmation" and he said he hadn't gotten to where he could play that one yet, but he kept working at it. It made me think of how many young jazz players routinely play that tune out of *The Real Book*, without really getting to the musical point of that tune.

approach, students learn each and every nuance of the solo, can sing it perfectly, imitating the feel and all the subtleties of phrasing with the recording and without it before moving on to learn it perfectly on their instruments. Imitating the time feel of great players is an excellent way to work on your own time feel, and I spent hours learning and imitating solos by Bud Powell, Lennie Tristano, Wynton Kelly, Bill Evans and Herbie Hancock (among others). It was always interesting working on a solo in this way. Initially, I usually felt that I couldn't play the lines as fast as the recording, but once I had worked on the solo a bit more, the technically difficult parts would get easier and then I often felt that I couldn't play as slow as the recording—relaxing and not rushing, getting the feel that the recording had. Anyway, for more on this, I would urge you to listen to Leibman's clinic DVD or seek out his transcription method in books he has written, because he is a great exponent of this approach and delivers it in a forceful, clear way that has great merit. It is one of the most powerful things you can do to improve your rhythm and to learn to swing.

Metronome Practice: 7 Tips

We've been speaking pretty generally about working with a metronome. Here are a few specific tips.

1 Try different ways of interpreting the metronome's pulse. For example, set the metronome so that the beats are as fast as it can go. This might be about 250. Now, interpret these as quarter notes at a moderately fast tempo. Play over this tempo. Try playing over different forms at this tempo: play over one chord, over a complicated tune and "free" without thinking about a pre-planned harmony. Play different rhythmic values, but include some 8th notes. Now slow the metronome down to half this speed, about 125 or so. Treat the beats as half notes on 1 and 3. Play over the same forms again, the one chord tune, the complicated tune and the free blowing. Try to use similar rhythmic values. How does it feel different from the previous 250 quarter note pulse? Now keep the metronome set at the same tempo and turn the beat around so that the pulse is now on 2 and 4. (If you have trouble interpreting the pulse as 2 and 4, say: "2,4,2,4,2,4" out loud and in time with the metronome beats, then add "1" between 4 and 2 and "3" between 2 and 4. Then you'll be saying "1, 2, 3, 4" but still feeling the strong beats to be on 2 and 4. Gradually, you

Tip #32 continued

This alto player hadn't been able to absorb the essence of that tune and really play it, play it as a deep musical expression the way Bird did. But he kept working at it, examining the tune in his practice. I think that to play jazz on a profound level, you have to spend time absorbing and working on things that don't all come together in a practice session. You have to spend time trying for something, listening for something. If you don't hear it this time, maybe you are setting the stage for hearing it in the future. It takes a certain kind of patience to keep at it. Needless to say, this isn't the direction that our fast moving information-oriented society is going in.

Practice tip #33
Rhythm is compulsive

What I mean by that is that we have a tendency toward certain tempos, toward certain rhythmic values at that tempo, toward certain rhythmic values in general. I remember a drummer telling me the story of a famous pianist he was recording with. It was a singer's date and she counted off a tune and they started playing, but the pianist stopped the take in the middle, saying the tune felt a little fast. The drummer, who was very familiar with the pianist's playing, instantly knew that the reason that the pianist wanted the tune slower was because he liked medium tempos at a certain speed where double timing felt good to him.

This pianist isn't alone in liking tunes at certain tempos. Most players call certain tempos more often than others. At certain tempos we have a tendency to play more triplets or more 8th note rhythms. These tendencies are all well and good. As I've said before, there is nothing wrong with a tendency. When you discover a tendency, one thing you might try is exploiting it, by which I mean developing it. If you play a lot of triplets at a medium slow tempo you might really try to work on that—can you add triplet rests in different places in the bar? Can you accent different triplets?

want to change this—let go of the accent on 2 and 4 and add the accents to 1 and 3. If this is difficult, concentrate on working with this for a while. Feeling the beat on 2 and 4 is an important skill. If necessary, slow the tempo down a bit and then gradually build it up to the faster tempo.) Again, play over the same 3 forms. How does this feel different? Does it feel better or worse to you? Alternate between having the beat on 1 and 3 and 2 and 4 until you can do either. Now slow the metronome down to half its speed again, about 62. Now interpret the metronome beat as 3 of the measure. This is exactly half time of half notes on 2 and4. Play over the three forms again. How does it feel to you now? We've had the metronome set on three different speeds, but the tempo we are playing hasn't changed, we've just been marking this tempo with progressively larger intervals of time. Generally speaking, using longer time values makes the playing feel more relaxed. Try other variations (see tip # 4 below)

2 Vary the tempos. When a musician says that a tempo feels like it's in the cracks, they mean that the particular tempo feels like an in-between tempo, a slightly unnatural tempo that is harder to feel. Everyone has certain rhythmic leanings. For everyone, a tempo feels fast at a certain place, maybe half note = 132. Maybe a medium tempo for you is about half note = 100 and slow, half note = 55. Wherever the spots are, there are certain tempos that you will tend to call more than others. Rhythm is very compulsive. Check out which tempos you are drawn to and which feel a little funny to you.

3 Try imagining. Set the metronome and just think the notes. Try to imagine how groovy they can be. How would you phrase them to make them swing harder? Without playing, without any of the technical issues that arise when you touch the piano, can you imagine a deep swinging feel to your imaginary 8ths notes? Can you imagine your 8th notes swinging like Sonny Clark? Wynton Kelly? McCoy Tyner?

4 Try putting the beat on unusual parts of the measure. At a slow tempo, interpret the pulse as beat 4 of the measure. If that is comfortable try beat 2. How about the "and" of 4? Try putting the metronome at different upbeats of the measure, changing back and forth.

Tip #33 continued

Then try the opposite (this is the forking path method of practicing). In this case, see if you can play the medium slow tempo with no triplets. Use only duple meter: quarter notes, 8th notes, 16ths. How does this feel? Probably it feels a little unusual to you and maybe a little less comfortable, maybe now you know why you didn't choose it earlier. If you become comfortable with these rhythms that weren't the first ones you chose, you will have expanded your sense of what's rhythmically possible for you at this tempo.

Rhythm is one of the places where our tendencies are most obvious. Triplets or 8ths? Do you start on the first beat in the measure? Are all of your lines long? Are they short? Are they about the same length? Do you begin each phrase in the same place in the measure? Very often these unconscious leanings completely define what we sound like, and yet we are unaware that we are in a rhythmic prison of our own devising. Again, the way to change this is first to become aware of your habits and then to see what you might want to add to your palette of available rhythms.

Practice tip #34
Your rhythmic personality

Living in New York from the mid 80s, I was very lucky to see Kenny Kirkland play live a lot of times. The first time I saw him play, I was enthralled. Every time he touched the piano it was grooving. Every comp, every solo was so well executed rhythmically, whether he was swinging at a fast or slow tempo, whether he was playing swing, salsa or funk. I was very interested in his playing and I listened to a lot of it, and yet my attempts to bring something of his rhythmic approach to my own playing were always unsuccessful. Then I started listening to his playing in a different way. I tried to ignore the pitches and the harmony and just concentrated on the rhythm. I transcribed some of these rhythms without the pitches.

5 Sing with the metronome. If I am trying to check out new rhythms or phrasing I will often just improvise singing 8th notes or triplets broken up in different ways. Singing, my tendencies to cadence in a certain part of the bar are less pronounced than when I am playing and habits are reinforced by muscle memory. After singing for a while, I'll try playing similar rhythms using a few pitches, or just one pitch. **(CD EXAMPLE 22: Improvising rhythms over metronome, sung and then played)**

6 Try playing in front of the beat. What does that feel like? Try laying back on the beat. What does that feel like? Which do you usually do? Can you imagine doing the opposite? Try to play more and more in front of the beat until you are rushing the tempo and playing faster than the metronome. Now settle back into the tempo and play less on top, gradually dragging the tempo down until you are playing slower than the tempo of the metronome. Speed up until you are back in time with the metronome. (This comes from John McNeil, I think.)

7 (Here's one from another great trumpeter, John Carlson.) Repeat the above exercise using the degree of swing feeling as the parameter that you are adding and subtracting. Play a medium tempo with straight 8th notes. Gradually make the first note longer. Make the first note a quarter note triplet and the second an 8th note triplet. Make it feel heavier until you are playing a dotted 8th note for the first note of the line and a 16th for the second note of the line. Now gradually reduce the length and the accent of the first pitch until you are feeling triplets and then straight rhythms. Repeat. Try to maintain a particular degree of swing feeling for a long time. What is the least amount of swing you can bring to an 8th note line that is still detectable?

Tip #34 continued

On a fast tempo, I noticed that he played half notes with and without anticipations more than I did, also more quarter notes than I did. Other differences accumulated: he played more heavily accented 8th notes, more groupings of five or seven 8th notes in 4/4, more rhythms that were turned around versions of each other (repetitions of the same rhythmic figure first on the beat and then starting on the upbeat); at slower tempos, he didn't rely as much on triplets as I did. Each of these things were things that I could try. Not for the sake of trying to become a copy of Kenny Kirkland, but to enrich the rhythmic dimension of my playing. You should notice that I was not copying his rhythms per se, but trying to understand something of his rhythmic approach, his rhythmic signature.

I had a Japanese student who wanted to learn to play "modern." When she played for me, her vocabulary was all very staid bebop material without a lot of surprises. I asked her if she had ever transcribed people like Herbie Hancock, Keith Jarrett, McCoy Tyner, and she pulled out a folder of transcriptions—each 8 to 12 pages long, each complete with left hand voicings written in. Why didn't it sound more like she had internalized any of the lessons of these modern players? We'll talk more about that below.

The Rhythm Pyramid

Sometimes people conceive of a pyramid of rhythms that require you to eat a lot of fruits and vegetables and less protein, especially the fattier kinds. Oh wait a minute, that's the food pyramid. The rhythm pyramid is about all the different rhythmic values that are available at any tempo. (I always mix those two up.)

You start with a whole note. The next level is 2 half notes, which divide the bar in half. The next level would be 3 half note triplets, which divide the bar into 3 units. Then quarter notes, which divide the bar into 4. If I keep alternating duple and triple meter, the next level is quarter note triplets, which divide the bar into 6, then 8th notes, which divide the bar into 8.

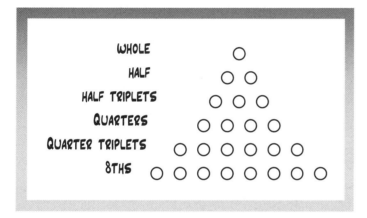

I can continue on to 8th note triplets, 16th notes, 16th note triplets and on and on ad infinitum, or at least until the units of rhythmic value get too small (too fast) for me to distinguish or play.

For a long time I have been practicing a variation of this idea. It is a kind of meditation for me and it goes like this. Set the metronome on a very slow tempo, 40 if that is the slowest, otherwise 30 or even slower. Try playing whole notes, meaning one note per beat, but try to feel them connected in a line. Try to feel the groove that results when you play one note to one beat. You can be in front or behind, don't bust yourself too much for this, just try to make the whole notes feel groovy. And notice your tendencies to drag or rush.

Next go to the next level of rhythm—the half note level. Again, notice your tendencies to drag or rush but focus on trying to make it feel good, to feel a groove with this level

Practice tip #35

What is swing?

Often I hear students whose swing feel is...well, clunky, for lack of a better word. Their 8th notes have a heavy swing feeling of alternating long and short notes, a little like one quarter note triplet followed by one 8th note triplet. This feel can sound a bit logy or corny. And it doesn't really account for the complexity and variety of swing feels.

Swing 8th notes vary from one musician to another and from one phrase to another within a solo. Double time (16th notes) at a slow tempo feels different from an 8th note line at a tempo twice as fast.

Generally speaking, students with uncomfortable swing feels overemphasize the unevenness of swing rhythm. At fast tempos, swing rhythms are almost straight. Indeed, sometimes it is more useful to think of swing 8th notes as straight with occasional accented notes.

Even at a slow tempo, 8th notes can vary between heavily swung triplet-feeling 8th notes or even the more heavily swung dotted 8th note/16th note 8th notes to almost straight. Wynton Kelly's classic solo on "Freddy Freeloader" *(Kind of Blue)* is a perfect example. The double time lines are pretty straight feeling, and he plays 8th notes in all the different ways described above, from triplet-y to straight. Herbie Hancock's 8th notes are often quite straight, but his approach to rhythm and articulation is quite varied. Kenny Kirkland's are usually straight and heavily accented (his articulation has a hard edge to it), as are Lennie Tristano's. Mulgrew Miller has a particularly wide variety in his 8th notes. Try to examine what sort of 8th notes your favorite instrumentalists use, and see if you can imitate them.

of rhythm, 2 notes to one beat. You can do this with a scale, or playing free or over the changes of a tune—try all of those and see what makes it easiest for this to feel like music to you, not just an exercise.

Then go to 3:1. This will feel like a waltz. Again, try to make it groove. You have to be very focused on small things for this to be useful—where is the front part of the beat, where is the back part of the beat and what feels good to you. After you feel that you are nailing this rhythm with a groovy feeling, go back to 2. Alternate. What happens when you switch from one to the other? Do you speed up or slow down—is it hard to find where the half notes are after you have been playing a lot of steady triplets? Again try to work on this until it feels natural and you can go from one groove to the other, locking into each groove as quickly as possible. Then go to 4 notes against a pulse. Repeat as you did with the 3:1 groove. Go between 4:1 and 3:1, first changing every 8 bars, then every 4 bars, then every two bars, 1 bar and within a bar. Go on to 5:1 This might feel a little unusual, since most of us aren't as used to subdividing one beat into five units as we are at dividing one beat into 4 or 3. Stay with the subdivision of five until that feels completely comfortable to you and groovy. Go back and forth between 4:1 and 5:1. Do you rush when you switch back to 4? Do you drag or rush the 5 when you switch from 4? Try to notice these tendencies without getting negative about them. See how quickly you can settle into the new subdivision. Now go to 6:1 and repeat all of the above steps, then 7, 8, 9 and 10, always spending a while locking in on the groove before moving on to switching between two neighboring grooves.

Now try to switch between grooves that aren't at neighboring levels of rhythm. So play the 2:1 or half note level and then try to jump to the 4:1 or quarter note level. What do you notice? How about going from 3:1 to 6:1? How about from 5:1 to 7:1? Try any combinations that you think are interesting, challenging or fun.

One of the great benefits of this exercise is that is helps you to notice all of the variations of playing in back and in front of all the different levels of rhythm. 5:1 is a little bit faster than 4 quarter notes and a little bit slower than quarter note triplets. 7:1 is a little slower than 8th notes and faster than quarter note triplets. When you try to feel different subdivisions of the beat, you are getting away from your rhythmic tendencies and you are exploring other ways to divide up the measure. Finally, it allows you to see what it feels like when you jump to different levels of rhythm. When you are soloing, you do this all the time, but perhaps before working on this exercise, you did it in a very unexamined way. Are you always hitting the time in a groovy manner when you have 16th notes, 8th notes and triplets in the same 4-bar phrase? Maybe the triplets are fine but the 8th notes are rushed.

There is another benefit of this exercise. Learning to feel where the 5, 7 and 9 subdivisions of the beat are helps you to play less mechanically. Lines can speed up and slow down, and you don't have to commit to an exact subdivision—your playing can be more gestural, more phrase oriented. Maybe a subdivision of 10 notes will feel like a smear of sound, and in that way it could be very freeing to experiment with a division of 10:1 if I am in the habit of playing machine gun 8th notes.

One might think that working on these rhythms is something that will lead in a "modern" direction, but these issues are beyond style. The greatest players—from Lester Young, Ben Webster and Johnny Hodges to Charlie Parker, Trane, Sonny Rollins and Bud Powell—are very free with their rhythmic approaches. When I do a lot of this sort of practice, I don't usually go on the gig and find that I am playing quintuplets and septuplets instead of 8th notes, but what I do find is that the beats in the measure—1,2,3 and 4—are clearer to me. They are wider, and I can be more free with the rhythms I play.

The ultimate goal of this kind of practice is to be able to play notes at any speed while you are feeling the time go by in a measured way. If you familiarize yourself with rhythms that are unfamiliar to you, these rhythms then become available to you when you are soloing.

The 8 Places 8th Notes Occur in a Measure

Now that we've explored all these different subdivisions, let's work on the opposite thing: 8th notes. 8th notes are extremely important in playing jazz. Even if you become comfortable with every odd number grouping over a pulse from 1 to 49 (that's easy, after all it's just 7 septuplets), you will probably still play a lot of 8th notes. The relationship of a quarter note pulse to all the places an 8th note can occur in a measure is of central importance for feeling swing rhythm.

Each of these 8th note slots in a bar of 4/4 has a different feeling to it. It's like hearing the color of scale degrees—the 3rd sounds major or happy, the 4th sounds even, kind of plain or austere; the 7th, edgy, pushing to resolve up (or whatever subjective associations you bring to your perception of the colors of scale degrees). Rhythmically, 8th notes are just as colorful: the 1 is the biggest resolution spot or "home," the 2 is offbeat, but strong, the "and" of 2 leans toward 3, 4 has a big flat early feeling, off beat and strong but more seated than 2. Again, these are my associations, whatever you feel is fine (as your therapist has no doubt tried to explain to you), but you want to strengthen your sense of the color of each upbeat and downbeat for you, so that you can feel them instead of counting them.

Here's an interesting way to explore this idea for which I am indebted to Kenny Werner. Pick some numbers, (about 3 or 4 numbers in every group of 8) between 1 and 32. Pick about an equal amount of odd and even numbers. For example: 1, 3, 4, 8, 9, 11, 14, 17, 20, 23, 26, 27, 30, 31. Now write the numbers 1 to 32 above the 4 bars filled with 8th notes.

After you have done that, wherever you have a number that is on your list, put an 8th note rest there.

You will get a random series of 8th notes this way. You can also reverse the pattern, putting 8th notes where you chose numbers instead of rests, and rests where you had 8th notes.

Since these are random rhythms, rhythms that you didn't choose, some of these rhythms will be groupings of 8th notes that aren't habitual to you. Try playing through these rhythms first with just a single note, then with two notes and then with the notes of a pentatonic scale. See if you can play through a blues using this rhythmic pattern or template, assigning new pitches each time but keeping the rhythms the same. With the reversed pattern, try playing these as a comping rhythm for your left hand on a slow blues working on this until you become comfortable enough to improvise over it. Or write an ostinato for your left hand that utilizes this rhythm. Practice improvising over the ostinato with half notes, quarters and combinations of 8th notes and rests. Start with a single pitch and add pitches as your comfort with the ostinato increases.

Rhythmic Transcriptions

Let's return to the Japanese student I spoke about earlier. Why hadn't she internalized any of the solos she had transcribed? It's always possible to transcribe a solo note by note without taking in the content of the music you are transcribing. We picked a solo that she had transcribed: Chick Corea's "Matrix" solo from *Now He Sings, Now He Sobs*. She had transcribed the whole solo but we only focused on the first two choruses. We ignored the pitches of the solo and she learned the rhythms in both hands. She started as we did with the random 8th-note exercise above, using just one pitch with each hand and gradually adding material until she was playing either 1 and 5 or diatonic 4th voicings from the C Dorian scale in her left hand and notes from the Eb pentatonic in her right. Now, she sounded like Chick Corea. She had learned something important and elemental about his rhythmic signature. Here's another example, a Kenny Kirkland solo from Bob Hurst's record *Presenting Bob Hurst*.

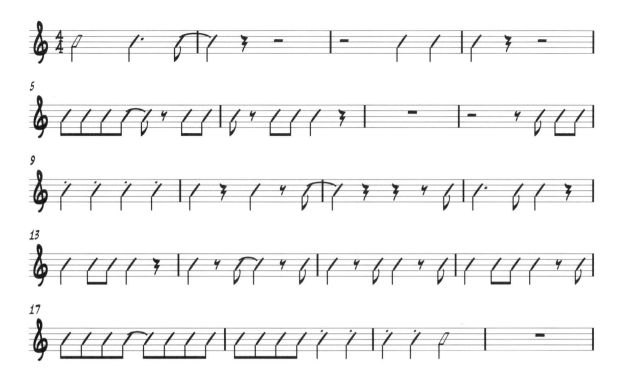

As I said before, it wasn't until I started analyzing the rhythms that Kenny Kirkland used, that I started to be able to get some of Kenny Kirkland's sound into my own playing. In a sense, I would say that it wasn't until I started transcribing his rhythms that I really heard what he was playing. These new rhythms gave me interesting new directions to work on in my own playing.

Odd Meter

Until I was in my mid 30s, I don't think I played in a meter other than 3, 4, or 6. I must have played "Take Five" at one point or another, and I think I transcribed the melody of "Blue Rondo a la Turk" when I was in high school, but that was probably the extent of my forays into odd meter until I came to New York in the 80s. One of the truly interesting things about being part of the jazz community is that the music continues to develop in surprising directions and so there are always new things to work on. Being part of a musical community, these directions aren't always things I would have chosen, but then once you are involved in the new area little by little it becomes an interest and eventually a passionate one. I never played in unusual meters when I was younger, because most of the music that I was listening to was in 4/4, 3/4 or 6/8. One of my favorite records, Wayne Shorter's *Etcetera,* had a tune in 5/4 ("Indian Song"), but this is a 5/4 with a constant bass ostinato and in terms of complexity a far cry from the odd meter playing of Brad Mehldau, Dave Holland, Steve Coleman, Achim Kauffman (a great German pianist) and others. Of course there were other odd-meter-oriented bands in the 70s and 80s, Mahavishnu Orchestra for example, but this music, while something I liked and enjoyed listening to, just wasn't on my radar screen for playing. The same is true for bands like Don Ellis or Dave Brubeck. It wasn't a direction that I was pursuing as a player.

So, as an outsider to this way of playing, I had to find ways to work on odd meter. It was foreign to me and so offered another opportunity to find new ways to practice in order to get comfortable in this brave new odd meter world.

I began practicing with what I knew and I started in 7/4. Playing different standards in 7/4 and especially concentrating on phrasing the melodies in 7/4 helps you to feel different cadence possibilities in this meter. In 7/4 there are certain rhythmic patterns that help you to hear the meter. Sometimes people refer to this as the "clave" of the particular meter, but this term is applicable only in the broadest sense of the word as a key or skeleton of the rhythm and shouldn't be confused with the Afro-Cuban clave.

I should say here, that I benefited a great deal from talking to peers about how to work on this problem. Some of the following material is drawn, either directly or indirectly, from talks with Dave Pietro and Donny McCaslin.

7/4: Rhythmic Pattern 1: 4/4 + 3/4

This is probably the simplest way to divide the bar of 7/4 for jazz players used to 4/4. It can be felt as 2 half notes and then 2 dotted quarters.

There are a lot of ways to practice the above pattern:

1. Play the pattern over a form, like the blues or a standard. In these contexts, usually two bars of 4/4 become one bar of 7/4 or a bar of 4/4 and a bar of 3/4. Play the chord in your left hand on the first beat of the measure and play notes from the chord scales in your right hand, keeping the rhythm exactly. Set the metronome fast, with each beat equaling one quarter note.

2. "Open up" one of the long notes in the bar. What I mean by this is that you replace the first half note with four 8th notes, keeping the rest of the rhythmic values the same. This allows you to feel the rhythmic pattern underneath the 8th notes as you play.

Open up each of the long notes—the second half note, the first dotted quarter and the last dotted quarter—in turn in the same way.

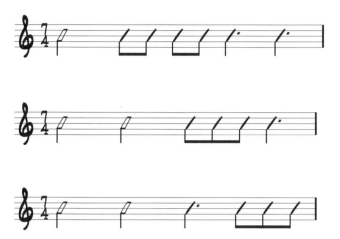

7/4: Rhythmic Pattern 2: 3/4 + 4/4

Of course, there are other ways to group a bar of 7/4. The next simplest idea is the opposite, a bar of 3/4 followed by a bar of 4/4.

Repeat all of the above exercises using this pattern.

7/4: Bars of 7/8

All of the other possible permutations of the dotted quarters and half notes have one thing in common: they divide the bar in half:

Since they can be divided in half, these patterns can be felt as 2 bars of 7/8.

The above pattern is probably the most common, although it is more often felt as two quarter notes followed by a dotted quarter:

This is a traditional rhythm that we see in a lot of Indian, Bulgarian and other Baltic folk music.

So let's go back to the 7/8 rhythm above. In 7/8 we will always be working with groups of 2's and 3's. (This is true for any odd meter: 9 can be 3,2,2,2 or 3,3,3. 11 can be 3,3,3,2 or 3,2,2,2,2. Of course, as we've seen above the 2's and 3's can then be moved around within the measure.) So, writing in all the 8ths notes for the above pattern gives us:

Note that we accent on the first 8th note of each group. A groovier, almost shuffle-like way to feel the above rhythm would be:

Practice tip #36
Bulgarian influences

I've been fortunate in a lot of ways, as I've already mentioned to you. (You just have to keep counting your blessings when you live the non-stop party that is my life.) One lucky thing I've experienced a lot lately is the opportunity to travel and come in contact with great musicians from other cultures. Unusual meters have come to jazz partially from world music influences, such as Indian classical music and Eastern European folk music.

I teach at a conservatory in Groningen in the Netherlands in a steady visiting professor capacity, going for a week every two months or so. This school draws students from all over the world: Russia, Romania, Sweden, the U.K., Korea, China, Lithuania, Italy, Spain, Portugal, Lebanon, Greece and on and on. Last year, I had a little time off in Groningen and I started playing with a group of Bulgarian musicians. This was very helpful for me since at the time I was working on odd meter playing for various bands that I was working with in New York.

For these Bulgarian musicians, odd meter playing is as natural as playing in 4/4 is for people from the United States. It is in their folk music—it is in the dance music they play at weddings and concerts, performed by gypsy musicians and virtuosi. One of the most well known Bulgarian musicians is the amazing clarinetist Ivo Papasov.

(Two great Bulgarian musicians were playing in New York and Michael Brecker was in the audience. After the concert, Michael came up to the accordion player in the band and asked him if he could take a lesson. The Bulgarian was not terribly interested and responded vaguely, saying he was busy. The other Bulgarian musician recognized Michael Brecker, and said somewhat abashedly, "Hey man, do you know who that was? That was Michael Brecker!" His friend responded, "So what? It's not as if it was Ivo Papasov!")

There has been so much interest

It's important to get beyond counting these groups of notes. It has to feel like short short long, short short long. The transformation from the 12 12 123 to the figure above makes the rhythm feel more relaxed, and we can feel the last two notes of the above pattern a little bit like the long short of two swung 8th notes.

So we've played 12 12 123 and short short long with a swingier, more relaxed groove. How should you practice this? I would sing these rhythms, clap them, play them between two hands, play them up scales: (using scale degrees. Start with 12 12 123, 23 23 234, 34 34 345 but then add any other scale permutations that allow you to assign pitches to the rhythms). You can play them over a form or just in one key. The next step is to vary the order of the twos and threes:

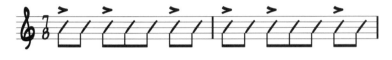

and

Again, these rhythms should also be played in the simpler short long short and short short long versions.

How about the metronome? When we left it last, we had it on quarter notes, but once we divide the bar into two bars of 7/8 we can set the metronome to a much slower tempo and feel it on the downbeat (first 8th note) of each bar of 7/8. Practicing all of the combinations of 2's and 3's in each odd meter helps you to feel that meter better and it also helps you to feel different groupings of 2's and 3's in 4/4.

Using the Metronome in Odd Meter Situations

With the advent of computers and sequencers in every notation program, most musicians have access to a way to construct odd meter bass lines and drum patterns over any form that you are working on. This can be useful. In addition to that, my DB 66 can play any pattern up to nine (meaning, an accent on 1 and then 8 clicks) and all of the combinations of 2 and 3, 3 and 4, 4 and 5 up to 8 and 9 or a bar of 17. (Although

Tip #36 continued

in Bulgarian music in the U.S. Bands like Dave Douglas' Tiny Bell Trio, Pachora and others have brought a lot of this music to the attention of new jazz audiences, although I have to admit, I was pretty slow to get hip to it. It was very interesting for me to meet musicians from Bulgaria who were trying to cross over from the other direction—from Bulgarian folk music into jazz.

Playing with these guys was fun because they made odd meter playing a lot less academic for me. Great jazz odd meter players often disguise the meter they are playing. Musicians like Dave Holland, Chris Potter, Billy Kilson, Tyshawn Sorley, and Steve Coleman are all brilliant at playing free rhythmically over odd meter. They play with the freedom in 7 and 9, and 13 that other people play in 4. But the Bulgarian approach is a little different. They were able to really rock these meters, freely switching patterns within the 7/8 but building the 8th note groove in a dance-like way. (To be sure, they are also capable of disguising the meter, but as a form of dance music, I felt a way into working on these grooves with Bulgarians that I hadn't really caught on to with American jazz musicians. With jazz players, I felt like I was too far behind the curve.)

(By the way, this school is quite good and very cheap by American college standards, due to government subsidy. For more information, visit www.newyorkgroningen.com.)

I have to point out, after each of these mixed settings, it has a rather useless setting for the numbers in reversed order, so after 2 + 3 comes 3 + 2 and after 4 + 5 it has 5 + 4 all the way up. These two settings are completely indistinguishable, except for what the metronome thinks is the first bar.) These are useful tools, but not nearly as useful as a traditional metronome.

Here are some ways you can use a regular (beats without any accents) metronome for odd meter. (We'll stick with 7 for purposes of convenience, but this is equally applicable to any meter.)

1 On all of the quarter notes in a bar of 7/4
This is the simplest conceptually. Tempos may feel a bit frantic.

2 On the downbeat of 1 in a bar of 7/4
This in effect becomes the same exercise as we did above, feeling various divisions of a beat—in this case the division of 7:1. You can vary this approach by making the beat occur on 2, 3, 4, 5, 6 or 7 as well, Then try placing on the upbeat for an even greater challenge.

3 In the middle of the bar (effectively splitting the 7/4 into two bars of 7/8).

As we discussed above. One interesting effect of this is that it allows you to feel any odd meter as duple, meaning divisible into 2 equal parts. For some of us, this is a big advantage, because we can feel the meter as a kind of 2/4 (and by extension, 4/4). This is the flip side of playing hemiolas in 4, and for some jazz musicians (like me), having spent a long time becoming comfortable playing complex rhythms in 4/4, I can feel groupings of 5 and 7 over the bar of 4/4 more naturally than playing in 5/4 or 7/4. Finding the midpoint of the bar allows you to look at odd meter more like the way you play in 4, measuring the 7s against some even subdivision of the meter.

4 As a half note in a bar of 7/4. If you feel half notes against the 7/4 bar, the accented beats change for each measure: **1**23**4**56**7**1**2**34**5**6**7**. The second bar (which in this case accents the weak beats) will feel "turned around" from the first, which accented the strong beats of the measure.

Practice tip #37

There is no such thing as straight 8th notes

There isn't really any such thing as straight 8th notes. When you listen to any kind of world music or folk music, you have to try to feel how it swings. I remember trying to play percussion at a party in Sao Paulo with some great Brazilian musicians and those 8th notes (well, really they are 16th notes because they write in 2/4 but the point remains the same, pulse is pulse) are far from straight. I have a book about Brazilian music somewhere and there are a lot of examples on the accompanying CD of people playing time with shakers, the pandera and other Brazilian percussion instruments. I loved to listen to the percussionist keeping time on the shaker. It swings so hard, in a way that is very hard for me to emulate. There is a little accent on the 1st, 4th, 5th and 8th 16th note in the 2/4 bar. Keeping this in mind really helps you appreciate the nuance of each country's music.

Being able to feel 7 against half notes, and to notice when you are on the strong or weak beats, without losing your place will help you internalize the feeling of being in 7 more strongly. Playing half notes over any odd meter has this same turning around effect. 3/4: 123123, 5/4: 1234512345

Cross Rhythms: What's Really Difficult About Odd Meter?

The last step above gets at the real difficulty of playing in odd meters. For me, the most difficult thing to feel in odd meter is rhythms that cross the barline. Playing hemiolas, or cross rhythms, is especially difficult because we are used to cadencing these cross rhythms in 4/4. Being able to cadence cross rhythms in the odd meter goes a long way toward grounding you in that meter and being able to play whatever you want.

It helps to write this out.

Here are the half notes we discussed above. Half notes are probably the easiest cross rhythms to feel in an odd meter, but of course they are by no means the only cross rhythms you can work on. Three 8th notes will provide another cross rhythm, one that resolves in three bars:

seeing these rhythms written out like this doesn't really help visualize the cross rhythm all that well—you have to think of where the 8th notes are in the bar.

1 and 2 **and** 3 and **4** and 5 **and** 6 and **7** and
1 **and** 2 and **3** and 4 **and** 5 and **6** and 7 **and**
1 and **2** and 3 **and** 4 and **5** and 6 **and** 7 and
1

So now we have the cross rhythms that occur at three eighths, and at a half note (or four 8ths). Both two 8ths and one 8th of course aren't cross rhythms—they are even subdivisions of the 7/4 bar. Six eighths, seven eighths and eight eighths aren't cross rhythms, at least not in a way that gives us any new information—eight eighths is the same as two half notes, six eighths is the same as two dotted quarters and seven eighths divides the bar in half, as we've already seen. Five eighths, however IS a valuable cross rhythm, cadencing every five bars:

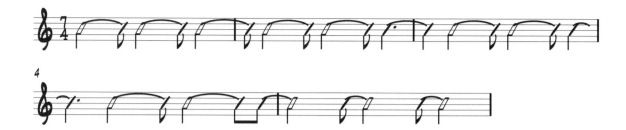

Once again, this is probably easier to comprehend if we subdivide at the eighth note level and accent every fifth eighth note:

1 and 2 and 3 **and** 4 and 5 and **6** and 7 and
1 **and** 2 and 3 and **4** and 5 and 6 **and** 7 and
1 and **2** and 3 and 4 **and** 5 and 6 and **7** and
1 and 2 **and** 3 and 4 and **5** and 6 and 7 **and**
1 and 2 and **3** and 4 and 5 **and** 6 and 7 and
1

Of course, the above hemiolas can be played in 4/4 as well.

In 4/4 there are interesting cross rhythm possibilities using three eighth notes (or dotted quarters; this is the most common cross rhythm in 4/4), five eighths, six eighth notes and seven eighth notes.

In the actual playing situation, I don't often play a cross rhythm for the whole seven bars or however long it is going to take for the cadence to resolve to one in the final bar. You want to be able to play cross rhythms for a bar or two—really, for any length of time—and cadence wherever you want. For this reason it's useful to practice the individual bars of the pattern separately; for example, in the cross rhythm of five eighths over 7/4, I might loop these bars:

1 and 2 **and** 3 and 4 and **5** and 6 and 7 **and** (repeat)
1 and 2 and **3** and 4 and 5 **and** 6 and 7 and (repeat)

and other combinations of bars as well.

Odd Meter Wrap-up

I want to add a few last thoughts about odd meter. For me, this is really a work in progress. What I mean by that is that this is an area where I continue to discover new approaches all of the time.

Let's quickly survey some of the areas that can be developed in our future practice on this topic:

1 Everything we've been working on has focused on the eighth note as the main subdivision. Go back and work out possibilities using triplets.

2 Subdivisions of the bar that generate non-eighth-note rhythms: Divide the bar into a bar of 4/4 and a bar of 3/4—you can try playing half note or quarter note triplets over the 4/4 bar and rest for the 3/4 bar. Then instead of resting, on the 3/4 bar play quarter notes, or dotted quarters. Rest for the 4/4 bar and play a 4 over 3 grouping for the 3/4 bar. Then instead of resting on the 4/4 bar, play quarter notes, half notes or half note triplets. Try other divisions of the bar such, as one bar of 6/4 and one bar of 1/4. Now play two 4:3 groupings for the 6/4 and nothing in the 1/4 bar. Or quarter notes in the 1/4 bar. Or eighth notes in the 1/4 bar.

3 Subdivisions of two bars that generate non-eighth note rhythms. Try these combinations of 14 beats (two bars of 7/4):8/4 + 6/4 (or 4/4 + 4/4 + 3/4 + 3/4) 9/4 + 4/4 + 1/4, 5/4 + 5/4 + 4/4, 4/4 + 4/4 + 4/4 + 2/4, 6/4 + 6/4 + 2/4 or any others that interest you. Play half note triplets whenever you have 4 beats and 4:3 whenever you have a three beat grouping. Or try other irrational groupings such as 5:3, 5:4. Write down some of your favorite combinations.

4 Now rewrite the above combinations in 7/4. This will give you over-the-bar groupings of half note triplets or 5:3 groups. Remember, you know what these things sound like from the above exploration of regrouping these bars.

5 Make sure you do simpler and more intuitive approaches as well, like singing, playing many melodies in different meter and of course listening to any odd meter music that you like.

The goal of all of this mathematical thinking is ultimately to be free in any meter and to be able to forget about all of the patterns and approaches. The philosopher Ludwig Wittgenstein said a similar thing about his writing. (This is a little heady, but bear with me. My nerd status was pretty much settled way back when I gave you the *Star Trek* sensor dress analogy.): "My propositions are elucidatory in this way: he who understands me finally recognizes them as senseless, when he has climbed out through them, on them, over them. (He must, so to speak, throw away the ladder, after he has climbed up on it.)" I hope something like that happens with this intense concentration on trying different mathematical not-always-intuitive approaches. In fact, the same thing could be said for all of the theoretical approaches I've suggested in the course of this book. These approaches should lead you somewhere, to something intuitive, interesting or fun. Then when you play, when you aren't breaking down a problem or trying to figure out how to play something you can't do or trying to get to know some rudiment in a deeper more immediate way, you need to forget the math, forget the theory, and play. Of course, if you never practice playing without thinking, you won't be able to drop these thoughts. You have to learn how to let yourself forget everything and just play, by spending time forgetting everything and just playing. Some time in every practice session should be devoted to that—dropping your hands on the keyboard and listening to the sound you make. Playing without judging, just listening and exploring.

Now let's leave the world of rhythm and focus on a problem that almost every student deals with at some point studying jazz.

CHAPTER 8: *Fast Playing*

T his isn't the first time we've discussed playing fast in the course of this book. It was lurking around the background of our "Giant Steps" discussion. It was there sneaking out from behind a lamp when we were talking about rhythm changes as well. But it is such an obvious problem that I think it's worth devoting a little space to this issue specifically.

There are a lot of reasons why playing fast might be difficult. If you are playing an up modal tune, you might feel that you run out of ammunition—that you don't have enough material available to you for lines (See chromatic approach notes and chord scale options.) There are the technical issues that playing fast raises—you may not have an efficient enough or relaxed enough technique to play eighth notes at a certain tempo. You may not be thinking fast enough harmonically on a tune with complex chord changes (See 100 steps on "Giant Steps.") You might turn the beat around, so that could mean that you haven't internalized the notion of keeping the metronome on 2 and 4 when you play (see metronome practice under rhythm). You might not be hearing the tempo, and you could be relying on muscle memory to keep you in time. You might have a tendency to cadence on 1 (or some other beat). You might have a difficult time leaving spaces rhythmically, or it might be difficult for you to use different rhythmic values. You might be trying to play chord changes that might be better left out at the faster tempo, meaning, you might not have found the deep structure of the form and so are locked into outlining each chord change in an unrelenting manner. You might have a tendency to play eighth notes with a very heavy swing feel and these heavy eighth notes get draggier and draggier as the tempo increases. It might be too technically difficult to play these uneven eighth notes at a fast tempo. You might prefer a certain type of articulation that causes you to have difficulty playing fast. You might find that when you try to play fast you tend to repeat yourself. You might find that when you try to play fast you tend to repeat yourself. (You probably saw that one coming.) You might find that when you try to play fast you rush. You might find that when you play fast your left hand and right hand get out of synch. You might find that when you try to play fast your ears aren't as engaged with what you are playing as when you play more slowly. You might think that when you play fast you have to play mostly eighth notes, or all eighth notes. You might think that when you play fast you have to feel the time a certain way and can't play half time. When you play fast, your left hand might be too loud.

The point is that part of figuring out how to play fast tempos is about trying to figure out where your problems with playing fast tempos are coming from.

Let's take a few of these and think about how to practice them intelligently.

Some problems come from not hearing the tempo, problems such as messing up the form, playing all eighth notes, articulation and rhythm issues that slow you down. Personally, I think this and technical issues are the biggest difficulties that students have playing fast tempos. I have a friend who is a bassist and occasionally studies with me. He had a big problem with playing fast tempos. When we discussed his ways of practicing, he admitted that he really only practiced one way: playing and singing lines of eighth notes at a slow tempo, and then gradually increasing the tempo. The only problem was that he never got past medium slow and he was frustrated in playing situations because he couldn't get any of the things he practiced out, the tempos were always too fast.

Here are the problems with that approach: 1) You don't play the same rhythms when you are playing fast tempos as you do when you are playing slower tempos, especially on the bass— at least, not all of the same rhythms. My friend said that he thought all of the great bassists had the chops to play all eighth notes at fast tempos. So we listened to bass solo after bass solo of great musicians, (I remember in particular, Larry Grenadier, Dave Holland and Scott Colley—I wasn't trying to stack the deck by playing bassists that aren't virtuosi soloists) and what we discovered was that even virtuosic bass players played a lot of rhythms longer than an eighth note at fast tempos. Of course, I am not saying that they don't have the chops to play all eighth notes. But not playing all eighths can be seen as a strength and not a weakness. The lines are more varied and interesting. The deep resonance of the instrument is served by some longer notes in the line. Extremely fast passages of low notes can be hard to hear. So, in this case the particular mode of practicing kept my friend from hearing something that could give him more options. Playing only slow tempos, he assumed, incorrectly, that solos on a fast tempo must be the same as solos over a slow tempo speeded up. 2) On an even more basic level, my friend had hit on a way of practicing that would never really help his problem with tempos. You don't get to hear the fast tempo if you never play it.

Another student had a problem with rushing fast tempos. This has something to do with getting edgy and nervous on fast tunes, but I think again that his practice technique was exacerbating the problem. He practiced mostly using the brute force method, setting the metronome on something that felt a little fast and gradually increasing the tempo whenever he could. He was really practicing how to rush, because he was always sending himself the message: a little faster, a little faster.

Practice tip #38
The diagnosis is... murder!

What is really going on in the example of my friend the bassist is that my friend hadn't diagnosed his difficulties well. He felt like he needed to gain more control of notes, improve his ears, get more conversant with scale options. All of these are certainly good goals for practice and no doubt something that he needs to work on, but in this case, these things alone were not enough to solve his problems with playing fast tempos.

I hear this sort of thing a lot, phrases like, "I can only get about 2 percent of what I practice out on a gig." I've heard that from some great players, but I don't really understand it. Maybe it's false modesty. Or maybe it's advertising. I mean, if you are only getting to 2 percent of your stuff, and you sound THAT good, just imagine if you could get another 5 percent out! Or 50 percent! That would be truly mind-blowing!

I think that your practicing should impact your playing much more than this. I think that if you are practicing and you aren't getting much benefit from it in your playing you may be practicing the wrong things, like my bassist friend.

Another student had technical difficulties that prevented him from playing fast. Personally, I feel that technical issues are often best addressed by a classical technique teacher. I've been to several terrific ones that helped me a lot. Pianists are fortunate because there is a long tradition of technical approaches to piano playing, and the technical issues of playing the piano haven't changed that much in the last 150 years or so. Electric bassists, jazz acoustic bassists and guitarists don't have the same tradition of technical study and repertoire available but all instrumentalists can benefit from finding a strong technique teacher to work with. Working with this student over time, I was able to help him analyze some of his inefficiency and work through many of his technical problems. In general, excess movement and over-emphasizing articulation and finger strength instead of relying more on the large muscles of the shoulder and forearms can be big problems.

So having diagnosed a few common difficulties let's get more specific about ways to improve fast tempo playing. Here are some options:

1 Brute force method: Set the metronome on a tempo that is difficult for you and play in as relaxed a manner as possible. Gradually increase the tempo. Yes, I know I said that I had a student who was teaching himself to rush using this method, but the problem there was an over-reliance on this one method more than anything else. It's necessary to have a simple way of working on the problem. So, keep setting the metronome faster. Pushing into tempos that you are unfamiliar with and playing in an unanalyzed sort of way is a valuable, if somewhat brute-force-oriented, way of hearing the faster tempo better. If you are working on tempos a lot, make sure that this isn't the only approach that you use.

2 Listening to the tempo. Put the metronome on a tempo that is too fast for you to comfortably play eighth notes, but not out of the realm of possibility. Imagine the lines you would play at this tempo if you could. Imagine starting in different places in the measure. Imagine starting on each downbeat and each upbeat. As you imagine it, try to release some of the stress you are imagining. Keep your breaths slow and relaxed. Sing some of the lines, not worrying too much about pitch, focus on the rhythms. Pick a line or two to play.

3 Learn several heads to rhythm changes, the blues or up modal tunes that are generally played at a fast tempo. Learn these at a fast tempo playing a bar or two at a time or using techniques 4 and 5 below.

4 Outlining. If you are having difficulty with a line at a fast tempo, try outlining. With this approach you play the first note of the line and the last note of the line. Fill in whatever happens on the 3rd beat, then 2nd and then the 4th beat. Now add upbeats, starting with the end of the measure, working your way to the front. Outlining helps you play the line by getting you to play the notes that fall on the strong beats first and then fill in the details later. Technically this is an extremely effective approach because, in order to play fast tempos, your hand should move toward groups of notes rather than single notes. Your hand needs to know which notes are important and then to tuck the less important notes into the line.

5 Here's a similar approach to working on a line at a fast tempo. Play the last note of the line, then the second to last note and the last note. In this way, keep working your way toward to beginning of the line. Do this without slowing down the tempo. This is a great exercise for a couple of reasons. One is that having the end of the line clear as a destination makes it easier to play the line—we have a tendency to ignore the ends of lines when we concentrate on learning each note consecutively. The other reason is that you are practicing finding each 8th note in the bar. First the 1, then the "and" of 4 and 1, then 4, the "and" of 4 and 1, etc.

Let's make this a little clearer. Here's the Bud Powell lick we looked at earlier.

play the last two notes

repeating it until it is effortless. Then play the last 3 notes

repeating these until this is effortless. Eventually, continuing in this way, you can learn the whole line playing it at a fast tempo.

6 Pick a fast solo to learn, just singing it. Don't even try to play it on your instrument. Learn parts of the solo so that you can sing them easily and comfortably, or the whole solo if you are enjoying it.

7 Make sure that you have analyzed the fast tune that you want to play very thoroughly and you have checked into possibilities of leaving out chord changes. If you are working on rhythm changes, for example, refer back to the deep structure that we talked about and see if it is easier to play the tune with that in mind, leaving out some of the changes to make blowing a little easier.

8 Try playing free harmony, up swing, no changes. This is extremely helpful. In keeping with the idea of practicing one focused thing at a time, it is good to separate harmony from rhythm. Sing rhythms at the fast tempo, then play some of those rhythms. Keep changing the pitches, keeping the rhythmic pattern. Limit the number of pitches you are using or improvise concentrating on a particular interval. Practicing without chord changes also helps you find the sounds that you are interested in independent of the harmony of any tune. If you do a lot of this kind of playing (which is valid in its own right), you have the added benefit of developing material that you will find uses for over songs. But for now we are more interested in the rhythmic dimension, so play any notes. Try hard to let yourself think of your instrument as a purely percussive instrument. **(CD EXAMPLE 23: Up-tempo free soloing)**

9 Listen to a lot of recordings of fast tempo solos. How fast is fast? Late 60s Miles Davis bands never played much faster than half note = 150 or so. Nowadays, some people play faster. How fast are your favorite fast songs? Know the answer to that. Also, like my friend the bassist, don't assume you know what people are playing at those tempos rhythmically. Check the rhythmic values and notice if the soloist is playing all eighth notes, or eighth notes with a lot of rests, or quarter notes or triplets. Maybe the way they are playing makes the tempo easier to play.

10 Articulation issues. Another reason students have trouble playing fast is because of either swing issues (DAH ba DAH ba DAH ba sorts of eighth notes) or articulation issues (heavy eighth notes that are extremely legato). The heavier sounding legato eighth notes sometimes happen to piano students that have listened to a lot to Keith Jarrett and Brad Mehldau. Obviously, both Keith and Brad have no trouble with fast tempos, but some students who are influenced by them and have exaggerated their articulation might. Many pianists play lighter and straighter at fast tempos. Check out McCoy, Herbie, Chick, Wynton Kelly, Lennie Tristano, Bud and others and often, if not always, their fast lines are lighter and less heavily swung than slower lines. This is equally true on any instrument. One way to think about playing faster is to think about holding on to the note for less time. You can demonstrate this to yourself by playing a line at a moderate tempo. (Put the metronome on 2 and 4 at somewhere medium around 100.) Play it a few times and memorize it, or pick a line from a solo or bebop head that you know already. Now play the same line with entirely straight eighth notes. Play it more and more staccato, leaving more space between the notes. What happens? For many students, as they straighten out the line and leave more space between the notes, the line will start to rush. Holding on to the notes too long makes it more difficult to increase the tempo. Keep in mind when you play staccato, you should try to do nothing extra with your fingers, just let go of the note. (For pianists, you should be feeling the motion in your whole hand, not doing anything special at the fingertip level, a little bit like dribbling a basketball.) Try to check if you are pushing the key into the key bed. This is extra effort that has no effect on the sound of the piano. Try to find the point in the key's downward movement where the hammer is tripped. You should be able to feel that. You need to push to that point and no further. Try to apply just the amount of force you need to make the note sound and then apply just enough effort to keep the key from coming up after the note has sounded. Practice this with a 5 finger exercise like the first Hannon.

For non-pianists, over-articulation can be a culprit for you at fast tempos as well. Try to do less, play the note more simply, with a straight tone.

Ultimately, playing fast is about hearing yourself in that tempo. I think it is important to be able to function in the situations you find yourself in, but also you should check out different pianists' approach to this issue. Thelonious Monk solves the problem of playing fast tempos in a different way than Keith Jarrett or Bud Powell or Art Tatum. Do some research and figure out what ways appeal to you. As a young player, the first pianist I listened to was Oscar Peterson. If that is your only role model, then you either need to listen to a lot more pianists or start shedding technique really hard. Hopefully, you can do both.

As we saw at the beginning of this chapter, the ability to play fast tempos is something that is aided by everything you are already practicing. Personally, I was surprised to find that when I started working on playing tunes in all keys, playing fast tempos got easier for me. Maybe some of you are already experiencing some of these unanticipated beneficial side effects in your own practice.

Still, whenever I am working on fast tempos I always try to do a lot of slow playing and ears-oriented practice to balance things out. I don't want my playing to become overly mechanical and exercise-like. I am reminded of something I once overheard Paul Bley say at a club. He had been touring with Steve Swallow and Jimmy Giuffre, playing a lot, and he felt that his technique was feeling so good that he was playing way too much with the band. I've heard a similar quote from Carla Bley, a tongue and cheek comment that she had gotten so much better as a pianist over the years that she wasn't even interesting to listen to any more. All this is another way of saying that, in the final analysis, it is a lot more important to be a great musician than a great pianist (or whatever instrument you play). To paraphrase an old ad campaign, it's not how fast you play it—it's how you play it fast.

CHAPTER 9: *Multi-Line Playing (on "Just in Time")*

Okay, this one is for the pianists out there. This is another aspect of jazz piano playing that has been getting more attention lately, due in part to the amazing degree of independence in multi-line playing that Brad Mehldau has been able to accomplish. While Brad's innovations in this area are significant, there is a long tradition of multi-line playing. We saw that the leading tones and separated bass function of stride playing had a multi-voice component, and inner lines and voice leading in the left hand is an important part of pianist's thinking—from Teddy Wilson, Duke Ellington, Art Tatum and Thelonious Monk to Bill Evans (whose rich densely chordal solo arrangements used inner lines inside voicings in a new way that set the stage for Keith Jarrett's innovations in this area), Keith Jarrett, Chick Corea and Brad Mehldau.

Personally, I have always been interested and attracted to counterpoint. I think this is true of a lot of jazz pianists. Maybe this has something to do with the place Bach inventions, fugues and preludes have in pianist's training—maybe this is a result rather than a cause: it may be that Bach particularly speaks to musicians of the present time period and so we end up incorporating Bach in a central place in our classical training.

As for styles discussed elsewhere in this book, I assume you are familiar with this kind of playing. If not, you should check out some of the solo work of the pianists listed above. Especially important in this area would be *Bill Evans: Alone* (or any of his solo recordings) and almost anything of the Keith Jarrett Trio (I am particularly fond of *The Cure, Tribute and Standards 1*, but I haven't kept up with all of his recent releases) and almost anything of Brad Mehldau's trio (again, my own favorites are T*he Art of the Trio 3: Live at the Village Vanguard and Places,* but you'd be hard pressed to find a trio CD of his that wasn't full of multi-line playing. Another excellent practitioner of the art is Fred Hersch, and you'd probably hear him using this texture most often in his solo recordings.

My own interest in this style of playing goes back many years. I was amazed when I first heard Keith's version of "All the Things You Are" on *Standards 1* with its intricate multi-voice playing on the introduction. As he continued to work with the trio format playing standards, solo interludes and introductions with complex counterpoint became an integral part of the texture of that band. I also remember being attracted to the kind of inner lines that Bud used in songs like "Cherokee," and amazing arrangements with lots of left hand independence and inner lines by George Shearing. I think it was something that I was always attracted to, but in a kind of unconscious way. I composed some arrangements that had a lot of counterpoint when I was a student at Berklee but I didn't have a way of integrating this technique into my playing and I shelved the idea for a while.

I found myself really getting interested in trying to play more counterpoint several years later. I took a lesson from Fred Hersch, and he opened up my eyes to some of the possibilities. Later, in my "Giant Steps" practicing phase, I found myself working on the idea of playing inner lines, and four voice playing over that form.

A few years later, I was in Japan, not performing this time, but staying with my wife, who was working there. I started going to a practice room daily, and it became a real retreat for me. (Practicing in a practice room, where there is no phone and no computer, in a country where you don't know anyone is a different experience from working at home. It's a wonderfully productive isolation, although a bit expensive in Japan.) During this period, I had several breakthroughs that helped me take this to another level.

So how do you start? Let's take the song, "Just in Time."

JUST IN TIME

COMPOSED BY JULES STYNE. LYRICS BY COMDEN AND GREEN

Perhaps the simplest way to start thinking about multi-line playing is to solo over the song.

(You can't get to this step if you aren't fairly conversant with playing chord changes. It would be a good idea to familiarize yourself with the changes of this tune using the techniques that we've applied throughout this book, involving chord scales, bebop scales, guide tone lines, chromatic approach notes, arpeggiation, intervals, singing, etc.—in short all of the things that we've worked on on the other tunes we've examined until now.)

This is one line, obviously, but if I want I can play it as a line broken between two hands.

If you practice doing this a lot, you will develop a sense of what these broken lines feel like. Different intervals are available to you, and your lines will take a different shape than if you were playing a single line. **(CD EXAMPLE 24: Soloing on Just in Time, one line divided between two hands)**

The next step is to add some sustained notes to the line.

This is much easier to do than to read. (At least for me.) Even though I have added some sustained notes, I am still essentially playing one line in that there is never a time when both lines move together. One hand plays, then holds a note while the other hand plays. Here's an improvised example of the same texture as above **(CD EXAMPLE 25: Soloing on Just in Time, one line divided between two hands with sustained notes)**

We could do something similar with the melody of the song. Let's play it in an ornamented way with the right hand.

Again, divide the line between your two hands; **(CD EXAMPLE 26: Melody and counterline, one voice at a time)**

Add the sustained notes to create two lines, as we did before. You should spend a long time on each of these steps, so that you get thoroughly comfortable with each one before moving on. Here's another improvised version of the above texture using the melody, a counterline and sustained notes. **(CD EXAMPLE 27: Melody on Just in Time, melody + counterline + occasional sustained note)**

Now let's work the same thing from a different angle. (For some of the ideas that follow I am indebted to Fred Hersch.)

4 Parts: SATB

1 Play the melody with your right hand and a second line in your left hand that is very close to the right hand as above. This is essentially a soprano melody and an alto counterline.

a   Make the alto counterline move in mostly quarter notes.

b   Make the alto counterline move in mostly eighth notes.

c   Play the soprano melody very strictly.

d   Play the soprano melody more freely rhythmically.

e   Play the soprano melody with ornamentation (still in quarter notes) with alto counterline playing mostly quarter notes (1:1 rhythmic relationship.)

f   Try to play the soprano melody with ornamentation (still in quarter notes) with alto counterline playing mostly eight notes (1:2 rhythmic relationship.)

g   Try to play the soprano melody with a little ornamentation in eighth notes with the alto counterline playing quarter notes (2:1 rhythmic relationship.)

h   Play the soprano melody with a little ornamentation in eighth notes with the alto counterline playing eight notes (1:1 rhythmic relationship.)

2   Repeat all of the above steps using only the right hand, playing the alto line with your thumb, 2nd and 3rd fingers and playing the melody with your 3rd, 4th, and 5th fingers (work it out, however you can). You will need to simplify your lines. Also, you may need to slow the tempo down to accomplish this.

3   Repeat the above steps down an octave. Start with two hands, the melody on top in the right hand and the lower line combining the counterline function with the bass function, so that the line will sound different than the alto line down an octave—functionally it is a different line and this line is played in the left hand. Then, as we did above, combine the two lines in the left hand.

4   Cross hands and play the melody in the left hand and chords in the right hand below the melody.

5   Uncross your hands and play the melody in the left hand and chords in the right hand above the melody.

6   Cross your hands and play the melody in the left hand and a counterline in your right hand below the melody.

7   Uncross your hands and play the melody in your left hand and a counterline in your right hand above the melody. How simple does the melody in your right hand have to be to keep from sounding like a new melody? Watch the volume in your right hand and try to sing the melody with your left hand below the counterline.

8   As another way of working on this, try doubling the melody in octaves. Double the counterline in octaves (improvising the counterline). Alternate the right and left hands and see if you can make your left hand sound as lyrical, with dynamics, phrasing and articulation that matches the right.

9   Play the melody in the right hand and play all eighth notes in the left hand.

This was a particular epiphany for me. I was in Japan practicing in that practice room (Yamaha Music Square Dogenzaka, Shibuya Tokyo, Room # 11, I think, although you should be able to practice in other places as well), and I realized that the most extreme left-hand-focused counterpoint that I needed to practice was all 8th notes in the left hand and the melody in the right.

What makes this hard? Well, for me, this particular step was hard because my ear tends to focus on the melody. Yes, I am playing 8th notes in my left hand and the melody in my right, but my ear is following the right hand. This isn't really surprising. We know that our ear is drawn to the soprano voice and when we are voicing chords (voicing in the classical sense of the word meaning choosing the relative volumes of different voices in a chord) it takes a lot of effort to make the inner voices more prominent than the soprano.

    a   This was my favorite step. Play the melody very slowly in the right hand. Play the eighth note line in your left hand, singing the left hand melody. I found this very difficult. So do less. Do the first bar and then start again. Do the left hand alone and then add just the downbeat of each measure in the right. Try to build it up to the point where you can sing the left hand line while you play the right hand melody.

    b   Cross hands. Repeat. (Bow to your partner, doe-si-doe.)

    c   Try it with the metronome. Try it with quarter notes in the left hand. Quarter note triplets. Try varying the rhythmic values in the left hand.

    d   Alternate playing one bar or two bar units where the left hand is playing the melody and the right hand is playing the line (mostly 8th notes) and the left hand, playing the melody with the right hand playing the 8th note line.

10 Let's look at all four voices now. We've played the melody in the soprano with alto counterline and we've played the melody in the tenor with the bass counterline. Play the remaining combinations of voices:

    a   soprano melody and the bass voice (there will be some counterline functions and some bass functions in the left hand line).

    b   soprano melody and tenor—the tenor line has some counterline and guide tone functions.

    c   alto melody with soprano upper counterline/guide tone line.

    d   alto melody with tenor (with two hands and with one hand).

    e   soprano melody with bass and tenor lines.

    f   bass and tenor lines without melody (this will be easier to try to do after you've tried to do the step before it, because you'll have a clearer idea as to the function of these lines).

    g   try playing three lines for a while. See if you can get all three lines to feel like. real voices, with strong melodies.

    h   play three voices without the melody: alto, tenor and bass.

11 Play four voices. Keep the melody in the soprano voice. Try playing primarily quarter notes in all voices. Try moving around eighth notes between the voices.

12 Play the melody in the alto, or tenor or bass with the other voices playing counterlines, guide tones or bass function.

13 Try moving around the melody from voice to voice within a chorus.

14 Try playing four voices without the melody.

15 Can you play this kind of counterpoint with a swing eighth note feeling? Play with metronome and without, adding and subtracting swing feeling to what you are doing.

Practice tip #39

Voices and the point of the chord change: not all of them need to get there at the same time

I think that one of the most interesting possibilities about doing this kind of counterpoint is that not all of the voices need to arrive at the chord at the same time. It's possible to get a kind of stretto feeling going in this kind of playing, with voices interrupting each other and with lines moving toward or away from chord changes in a free manner. This is particularly effective when you are playing a tune with a busy harmonic rhythm like "Giant Steps."

(CD EXAMPLES 28 & 29: 4-voices on "Giant Steps")

If you've gotten this far with the counterpoint, hopefully you are starting to feel your way and develop ideas of your own. For me, playing four voices over a form always feels a little bit like juggling—juggling lines, melodies and harmony. Also, there is a lot of illusion in playing these lines—as we saw from breaking up a single line between two hands. I also tend to experiment with the amount of 8th note subdivision I want in these lines. I can play all four voice chords with all the notes struck simultaneously (essentially the blockiest and least counterpoint-oriented way of playing) but if I am thinking about the movement of the inner lines, the horizontal dimension of these vertical chords, then I will play the same notes differently. Similarly, if I am playing eighth notes in all of the voices, then sometimes the accompanying lines are so limited (as compared to the moving lines) that I lose the sense of four-part independence that I am striving for. In all of these examples, listening will move you along the path. How does Bach do it? Look at the rhythms of lines in fugues, preludes and chorales. How about Fred Hersch, Bill Evans, Keith Jarrett, Brad Mehldau? What makes a line sound like a counterline and what makes it sound more functional, like a bass line or ostinato?

Other Interesting Piano Textures

Another interesting texture to follow up on is the doubling of lines in octaves in both hands that that we mentioned earlier. Obviously, this can be developed to an amazing degree, as players like Geoff Keezer, Oscar Peterson and Phineas Newborn Jr. demonstrate.

Octaves are only one interval that these parallel lines can be played in. Try playing lines in 4ths, 5ths, whatever intervals appeal to you. Then there is contrary motion. How about contrary motion in different rhythmic values? (I'm thinking specifically of a passage from Herbie's solo on "All of You": right hand plays an ascending diminished scale in broken 3rds in 8th note triplets and the left hand is playing a descending chromatic scale in quarter note triplets.) The possibilities are pretty much endless.

But this book isn't endless.

CHAPTER 10: *Conclusions*

W̲e've covered most of what we set out to work on. Let's review our initial list of practice issues:

1 Chord change spelling
   a using scales including bebop scales
   b using arpeggios
   c using chromatic approach notes
   d using guide tone lines

2 Playing over complex chord progressions
   a modulatatory forms (like Body and Soul)
   b "Giant Steps" (a specific variant of the modulatory sort of tune)
   c forms with lots of alternate possibilities (such as rhythm changes)

3 Playing fast tempos

4 Ear training

5 Creating more interesting left hand comps
   a rhythmically
   b harmonically/melodically

6 Improving metronomic time and developing a deeper groove

7 Playing odd meters

8 Playing better in all keys

9 Developing a personal voice

10 Adding new material to your linear vocabulary
   a intervallically
   b rhythmically
   c harmonically

11 Piano textures:
   a multi-line playing and inner lines in chordal passages
   b stride
   c bass lines

We've covered these topics—some in more detail and some in less. Some of them we have addressed directly and broken them down into exercises; some of them we have addressed more indirectly by working on a specific tune or in some practice tip. Now would be a good time for you to think about your own list of practice issues. What haven't we addressed that you feel is an area that you'd like to develop further?

After all we've been through, I hope that you have a better idea of how to come up with ways to address these problems. Try to keep these points in mind:

1 Break up each larger problem into the smallest, simplest things that you can practice. So if, for example, you want to play over a hard tune, do less. Play the roots only. Play the melody only. Play 2 bars of the form. Play half notes over the whole tune. Play slowly. Play the roots and sing melodies.

2 Use all your methods of comprehension. Try using many different approaches to a problem that each stress different skills. So, on the above-mentioned hard tune, sing roots and lines and functions of the chords (1, 3, 5, 7, 9, 11, 13) for an ears-oriented approach. Play the big scale, little scale, diatonic sevenths, guide tones, bebop scales and chromatic approach notes for a more theoretical approach. Try various rhythmic approaches, including different rhythmic patterns, the rhythmic pyramid, different metronomic approaches, different meters and different degrees of swing, different parts of the beat (front and back), etc. Try composing some choruses over the form. Try playing in all keys.

3 Monitor your level of engagement with your practicing. When you are bored with what you are practicing, move on to another approach, or to another tune. Make it fun.

4 Practice what's easy. Shoot for effortlessness. You haven't internalized things that are still difficult for you.

5 Try to keep developing your sense of what is interesting to you. Finding your voice is about learning what intervals, harmonies and rhythms are appealing to you. Don't be a passive practicer. Go out and find the music that excites you, and look inside yourself for interests that you want to see grow.

6 Try to be aware of tendencies and habits. Try to develop things that you habitually play and also try to practice things that are the opposite of what is habitual. Use the forking path method to become more analytical about what you are practicing.

7 Don't confuse humility for self-depreciation. I said earlier that humility is important for practicing because it allows you to recognize areas that could use work in your playing. But humility doesn't mean running yourself down as you practice. Improvising takes a lot of self-assertion. A large part of having good time is being strong about where you hear the time in a band. A lot of students tend to have a negative internal monologue going as they practice or play. This only slows down your rate of improvement.

I hope you practice better, with more enjoyment or more productively as a result of these ideas. I'm going to leave you with two more quick stories. One is from a Jimmy Heath clinic. I was called to play with a big band at a school where I used to teach, because they didn't have a pianist at the school that could read his arrangements (a bad sign). Anyway, Jimmy Heath came to the school and the students (a fairly uncommitted group of slackers in this instance, to be brutal but honest) pretty much murdered his charts for about 40 minutes. Jimmy Heath soloed over the tunes and kept quiet about the mistakes. They were going to count off one more when he stopped the band. "How many of you practiced today?" he asked. (It was a late morning clinic that had started at 11:00 or so.) One or two students raised their hands. "Well, I practiced today before I came here," he said. "and I am 72 years old and I practice every day. When I go home I am going to practice some more." Then he showed the students what he was working on.

For me, Jimmy Heath's clinic was truly inspiring. Practicing is really one of the most exciting aspects of music. The exploration continues and, speaking from personal experience, it gets better and more interesting as I go. When I was in my 20s, I moved to Boston to study with a well-known teacher there, and I was trying to practice as much as I could stand. I ended up getting tendonitis, and one of the things that I learned was that I wasn't a good enough practicer to do it for eight hours at a stretch. Now it's getting better and the hours pass by, and I am really engaged with what I am doing in a way that I wasn't when I was younger.

I have heard a rumor that Sonny Rollins used to keep or perhaps still keeps a practice journal. The rumor goes that there are 28 volumes of it and someday it'll get published. There's something very life-affirming about that, if it's true, and if it isn't I'd just as soon pretend that it is. Of course, Sonny Rollins' whole career and way of playing is inspiring and whether or not he wrote down notes as he worked on things isn't really important, because we have his recordings and we can still hear him play. But I derive a lot of inspiration from the fact that practicing is something that we all do, all of us musicians. We sit with our instruments and spend time thinking about what we could play on them and working on things to help us play better.

I guess that is why it's always so inspiring to hear a tape of one of your musical heroes practicing. There's a famous one of Clifford Brown playing "Cherokee" and another that's come out on CD of Monk working on "Round Midnight" for about 20 minutes at a club: pausing, playing, searching for a chord, talking a little and then starting again. This is the other side of that mad genius stuff we see so often in the media. Even the film, *Straight No Chaser,* great as it is, gives us the image of a crazy genius. I know that that's only a part of the story, because when you hear Monk practicing, you can hear that it's about focus and searching as much, if not more, than mad inspiration. It's about practicing.

It's funny. The media understand musicians so poorly that almost every story about musical heroes ends up with the artist transmitting his genius in a kind of elated super human outpouring. For me, the more inspiring story is the human process of working, exploring and, ultimately, learning.

Good luck with your practicing.

David Berkman

Sher Music Co. — The finest in Jazz & Latin Publications

THE NEW REAL BOOK SERIES

The Standards Real Book (C, Bb or Eb)

A Beautiful Friendship	Days Of Wine And Roses	I Only Have Eyes For You	Old Folks	Summer Night
A Time For Love	Dreamsville	I'm A Fool To Want You	On A Clear Day	Summertime
Ain't No Sunshine	Easy To Love	Indian Summer	Our Love Is Here To Stay	Teach Me Tonight
Alice In Wonderland	Embraceable You	It Ain't Necessarily So	'Round Midnight	That Sunday, That Summer
All Of You	Falling In Love With Love	It Never Entered My Mind	Secret Love	The Girl From Ipanema
Alone Together	From This Moment On	It's You Or No One	September In The Rain	Then I'll Be Tired Of You
At Last	Give Me The Simple Life	Just One Of Those Things	Serenade In Blue	There's No You
Baltimore Oriole	Have You Met Miss Jones?	Love For Sale	Shiny Stockings	Time On My Hands
Bess, You Is My Woman	Hey There	Lover, Come Back To Me	Since I Fell For You	'Tis Autumn
Bluesette	I Can't Get Started	The Man I Love	So In Love	Where Or When
But Not For Me	I Concentrate On You	Mr. Lucky	So Nice (Summer Samba)	Who Cares?
Close Enough For Love	I Cover The Waterfront	My Funny Valentine	Some Other Time	With A Song In My Heart
Crazy He Calls Me	I Love You	My Heart Stood Still	Stormy Weather	You Go To My Head
Dancing In The Dark	I Loves You Porgy	My Man's Gone Now	The Summer Knows	**And Hundreds More!**

The New Real Book - Volume 1 (C, Bb or Eb)

Angel Eyes	Eighty One	I Thought About You	My Shining Hour	Shaker Song
Anthropology	E.S.P.	If I Were A Bell	Nature Boy	Skylark
Autumn Leaves	Everything Happens To Me	Imagination	Nefertiti	A Sleepin' Bee
Beautiful Love	Feel Like Makin' Love	The Island	Nothing Personal	Solar
Bernie's Tune	Footprints	Jersey Bounce	Oleo	Speak No Evil
Blue Bossa	Four	Joshua	Once I Loved	St. Thomas
Blue Daniel	Four On Six	Lady Bird	Out Of This World	Street Life
But Beautiful	Gee Baby Ain't I Good	Like Someone In Love	Pent Up House	Tenderly
Chain Of Fools	To You	Little Sunflower	Portrait Of Tracy	These Foolish Things
Chelsea Bridge	Gone With The Wind	Lush Life	Put It Where You Want It	This Masquerade
Compared To What	Here's That Rainy Day	Mercy, Mercy, Mercy	Robbin's Nest	Three Views Of A Secret
Darn That Dream	I Love Lucy	The Midnight Sun	Ruby, My Dear	Waltz For Debby
Desafinado	I Mean You	Monk's Mood	Satin Doll	Willow Weep For Me
Early Autumn	I Should Care	Moonlight In Vermont	Search For Peace	**And Many More!**

The New Real Book Play-Along CDs (For Volume 1)

CD #1 - Jazz Classics - Lady Bird, Bouncin' With Bud, Up Jumped Spring, Monk's Mood, Doors, Very Early, Eighty One, Voyage **& More!**
CD #2 - Choice Standards - Beautiful Love, Darn That Dream, Moonlight In Vermont, Trieste, My Shining Hour, I Should Care **& More!**
CD #3 - Pop-Fusion - Morning Dance, Nothing Personal, La Samba, Hideaway, This Masquerade, Three Views Of A Secret, Rio **& More!**
World-Class Rhythm Sections, featuring Mark Levine, Larry Dunlap, Sky Evergreen, Bob Magnusson, Keith Jones, Vince Lateano & Tom Hayashi

The New Real Book - Volume 2 (C, Bb or Eb)

Afro-Centric	Django	I'm Glad There Is You	Nica's Dream	Stablemates
After You've Gone	Equinox	Impressions	Once In A While	Stardust
Along Came Betty	Exactly Like You	In Your Own Sweet Way	Perdido	Sweet And Lovely
Bessie's Blues	Falling Grace	It's The Talk Of The Town	Rosetta	That's All
Black Coffee	Five Hundred Miles High	Jordu	Sea Journey	There Is No Greater Love
Blues For Alice	Freedom Jazz Dance	Killer Joe	Senor Blues	'Til There Was You
Body And Soul	Giant Steps	Lullaby Of The Leaves	September Song	Time Remembered
Bolivia	Harlem Nocturne	Manha De Carneval	Seven Steps To Heaven	Turn Out The Stars
The Boy Next Door	Hi-Fly	The Masquerade Is Over	Silver's Serenade	Unforgettable
Bye Bye Blackbird	Honeysuckle Rose	Memories Of You	So Many Stars	While We're Young
Cherokee	I Hadn't Anyone 'Til You	Moment's Notice	Some Other Blues	Whisper Not
A Child Is Born	I'll Be Around	Mood Indigo	Song For My Father	Will You Still Be Mine?
Cold Duck Time	I'll Get By	My Ship	Sophisticated Lady	You're Everything
Day By Day	Ill Wind	Naima	Spain	**And Many More!**

The New Real Book - Volume 3 (C, Bb, Eb or Bass clef)

Actual Proof	Dolphin Dance	I Hear A Rhapsody	Maiden Voyage	Speak Like A Child
Ain't That Peculiar	Don't Be That Way	If You Could See Me Now	Moon And Sand	Spring Is Here
Almost Like Being In Love	Don't Blame Me	In A Mellow Tone	Moonglow	Stairway To The Stars
Another Star	Emily	In A Sentimental Mood	My Girl	Star Eyes
Autumn Serenade	Everything I Have Is Yours	Inner Urge	On Green Dolphin Street	Stars Fell On Alabama
Bird Of Beauty	For All We Know	Invitation	Over The Rainbow	Stompin' At The Savoy
Black Nile	Freedomland	The Jitterbug Waltz	Prelude To A Kiss	Sweet Lorraine
Blue Moon	The Gentle Rain	Just Friends	Respect	Taking A Chance On Love
Butterfly	Get Ready	Just You, Just Me	Ruby	This Is New
Caravan	A Ghost Of A Chance	Knock On Wood	The Second Time Around	Too High
Ceora	Heat Wave	The Lamp Is Low	Serenata	(Used To Be A) Cha Cha
Close Your Eyes	How Sweet It Is	Laura	The Shadow Of Your Smile	When Lights Are Low
Creepin'	I Fall In Love Too Easily	Let's Stay Together	So Near, So Far	You Must Believe In Spring
Day Dream	I Got It Bad	Lonely Woman	Solitude	**And Many More!**

The All Jazz Real Book

Over 540 pages of tunes as recorded by: Miles, Trane, Bill Evans, Cannonball, Scofield, Brecker, Yellowjackets, Bird, Mulgrew Miller, Kenny Werner, MJQ, McCoy Tyner, Kurt Elling, Brad Mehldau, Don Grolnick, Kenny Garrett, Patitucci, Jerry Bergonzi, Stanley Clarke, Tom Harrell, Herbie Hancock, Horace Silver, Stan Getz, Sonny Rollins, and MORE!

Includes a free CD of many of the melodies (featuring Bob Sheppard & Friends). $44 list price. Available in C, Bb, Eb

The European Real Book

An amazing collection of some of the greatest jazz compositions ever recorded! Available in C, Bb and Eb. $40

• Over 100 of Europe's best jazz writers.
• 100% accurate, composer-approved charts.
• 400 pages of fresh, exciting sounds from virtually every country in Europe.
• Sher Music's superior legibility and signature calligraphy makes reading the music easy.

Listen to FREE MP3 FILES of many of the songs at www.shermusic.com!

See **www.shermusic.com** for more information, including a complete list of tunes in all our fake books.
To order, call (800) 444-7437 or fax (707) 763-2038

SHER MUSIC JAZZ PUBLICATIONS

The Real Easy Book Vol. 1
TUNES FOR BEGINNING IMPROVISERS

Published by Sher Music Co. in conjunction with the Stanford Jazz Workshop. $22 list price.

The easiest tunes from Horace Silver, Eddie Harris, Freddie Hubbard, Red Garland, Sonny Rollins, Cedar Walton, Wes Montgomery Cannonball Adderly, etc. Get yourself or your beginning jazz combo sounding good right away with the first fake book ever designed for the beginning improviser.
Available in C, Bb, Eb and Bass Clef.

The Real Easy Book Vol. 2
TUNES FOR INTERMEDIATE IMPROVISERS

Published by Sher Music Co. in conjunction with the Stanford Jazz Workshop. Over 240 pages. $29.

The best intermediate-level tunes by: Charlie Parker, John Coltrane, Miles Davis, John Scofield, Sonny Rollins, Horace Silver, Wes Montgomery, Freddie Hubbard, Cal Tjader, Cannonball Adderly, and more! Both volumes feature instructional material tailored for each tune. Perfect for jazz combos!
Available in C, Bb, Eb and Bass Clef.

The Real Easy Book Vol. 3
A SHORT HISTORY OF JAZZ

Published by Sher Music Co. in conjunction with the Stanford Jazz Workshop. Over 200 pages. $25.

History text and tunes from all eras and styles of jazz. Perfect for classroom use. Available in C, Bb, Eb and Bass Clef versions.

The Best of Sher Music Co. Real Books
100+ TUNES YOU NEED TO KNOW

A collection of the best-known songs from the world leader in jazz fake books – Sher Music Co.!

Includes songs by: Miles Davis, John Coltrane, Bill Evans, Duke Ellington, Antonio Carlos Jobim, Charlie Parker, John Scofield, Michael Brecker, Weather Report, Horace Silver, Freddie Hubbard, Thelonious Monk, Cannonball Adderley, and many more!

$26. Available in C, Bb, Eb and Bass Clef.

The Serious Jazz Book II
THE HARMONIC APPROACH

By Barry Finnerty, Endorsed by: Joe Lovano, Jamey Aebersold, Hubert Laws, Mark Levine, etc.

- A 200 page, exhaustive study of how to master the harmonic content of songs.
- Contains explanations of every possible type of chord that is used in jazz.
- Clear musical examples to help achieve real harmonic control over melodic improvisation.
- For any instrument. $32. Money back gurantee!

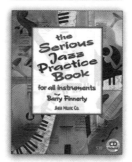

The Serious Jazz Practice Book By Barry Finnerty

A unique and comprehensive plan for mastering the basic building blocks of the jazz language. It takes the most widely-used scales and chords and gives you step-by-step exercises that dissect them into hundreds of cool, useable patterns.
Includes CD - $30 list price.

"The book I've been waiting for!" – Randy Brecker.

"The best book of intervallic studies I've ever seen."
– Mark Levine

The Jazz Theory Book

By Mark Levine, the most comprehensive Jazz Theory book ever published! $38 list price.
- Over 500 pages of text and over 750 musical examples.
- Written in the language of the working jazz musician, this book is easy to read and user-friendly. At the same time, it is the most comprehensive study of jazz harmony and theory ever published.
- Mark Levine has worked with Bobby Hutcherson, Cal Tjader, Joe Henderson, Woody Shaw, and many other jazz greats.

Jazz Piano Masterclass With Mark Levine "THE DROP 2 BOOK"

The long-awaited book from the author of "The Jazz Piano Book!" A complete study on how to use "drop 2" chord voicings to create jazz piano magic! 68 pages, plus CD of Mark demonstrating each exercise. $19 list.

"Will make you sound like a real jazz piano player in no time." – Jamey Aebersold

Metaphors For The Musician
By Randy Halberstadt

This practical and enlightening book will help any jazz player or vocalist look at music with "new eyes." Designed for any level of player, on any instrument, "Metaphors For The Musician" provides numerous exercises throughout to help the reader turn these concepts into musical reality.

Guaranteed to help you improve your musicianship. 330 pages – $29 list price. Satisfaction guaranteed!

The Jazz Musicians Guide To Creative Practicing
By David Berkman

Finally a book to help musicians use their practice time wisely! Covers tune analysis, breaking hard tunes into easy components, how to swing better, tricks to playing fast bebop lines, and much more! 150+pages, plus CD. $29 list.

"Fun to read and bursting with things to do and ponder." – Bob Mintzer

The 'Real Easy' Ear Training Book
By Roberta Radley

For all musicians, regardless of instrument or experience, this is the most comprehensive book on "hearing the changes" ever published!
- Covers both beginning and intermediate ear training exercises.
- Music Teachers: You will find this book invaluable in teaching ear training to your students.

Book includes 168 pages of instructional text and musical examples, plus two CDs! $29 list price.

The Jazz Singer's Guidebook By David Berkman
A COURSE IN JAZZ HARMONY AND SCAT SINGING FOR THE SERIOUS JAZZ VOCALIST

A clear, step-by-step approach for serious singers who want to improve their grasp of jazz harmony and gain a deeper understanding of music fundamentals.

This book will change how you hear music and make you a better singer, as well as give you the tools to develop your singing in directions you may not have thought possible.

$26 – includes audio CD demonstrating many exercises.

The Latin Real Book (C, Bb or Eb)

The only professional-level Latin fake book ever published!
Over 570 pages. Detailed transcriptions exactly as recorded by:

Ray Barretto	Arsenio Rodriguez	Manny Oquendo	Ivan Lins
Eddie Palmieri	Tito Rodriguez	Puerto Rico All-Stars	Djavan
Fania All-Stars	Orquesta Aragon	Issac Delgaldo	Tom Jobim
Tito Puente	Beny Moré	Ft. Apache Band	Toninho Horta
Ruben Blades	Cal Tjader	Dave Valentin	Joao Bosco
Los Van Van	Andy Narell	Paquito D'Rivera	Milton Nascimento
NG La Banda	Mario Bauza	Clare Fischer	Leila Pinheiro
Irakere	Dizzy Gilllespie	Chick Corea	Gal Costa
Celia Cruz	Mongo Santamaria	Sergio Mendes	**And Many More!**

The Latin Real Book Sampler CD

12 of the greatest Latin Real Book tunes as played by the original artists: Tito Puente, Ray Barretto, Andy Narell, Puerto Rico Allstars, Bacacoto, etc.

$16 list price. Available in U.S.A. only.

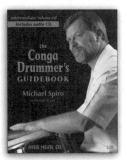

The Conga Drummer's Guidebook By Michael Spiro

Includes CD - $28 list price. The only method book specifically designed for the intermediate to advanced conga drummer. It goes behind the superficial licks and explains how to approach any Afro-Latin rhythm with the right feel, so you can create a groove like the pros!.

"This book is awesome. Michael is completely knowledgable about his subject."
— Dave Garibaldi

"A breakthrough book for all students of the conga drum."
— Karl Perazzo

Introduction to the Conga Drum - DVD
By Michael Spiro

For beginners, or anyone needing a solid foundation in conga drum technique.

Jorge Alabe – "Mike Spiro is a great conga teacher. People can learn real conga technique from this DVD."

John Santos – "A great musician/teacher who's earned his stripes"

1 hour, 55 minutes running time. $25.

Muy Caliente!

Afro-Cuban Play-Along CD and Book
Rebeca Mauleón - Keyboard
Oscar Stagnaro - Bass
Orestes Vilató - Timbales
Carlos Caro - Bongos
Edgardo Cambon - Congas
Over 70 min. of smokin' Latin grooves!
Stereo separation so you can eliminate the bass or piano. Play-along with a rhythm section featuring some of the top Afro-Cuban musicians in the world! $18.

The True Cuban Bass

By Carlos Del Puerto, (bassist with Irakere) and **Silvio Vergara**, $22.

For acoustic or electric bass; English and Spanish text; Includes CDs of either historic Cuban recordings or Carlos playing each exercise; Many transcriptions of complete bass parts for tunes in different Cuban styles – the roots of Salsa.

101 Montunos
By Rebeca Mauleón

The only comprehensive study of Latin piano playing ever published.

- Bi-lingual text (English/Spanish)
- 2 CDs of the author demonstrating each montuno
- Covers over 100 years of Afro-Cuban styles, including the danzón, guaracha, mambo, merengue and songo—from Peruchin to Eddie Palmieri. $28

The Salsa Guide Book
By Rebeca Mauleón

The only complete method book on salsa ever published! 260 pages. $25.

Carlos Santana – "A true treasure of knowledge and information about Afro-Cuban music."
Mark Levine, author of The Jazz Piano Book. – "This is the book on salsa."
Sonny Bravo, pianist with Tito Puente – "This will be the salsa 'bible' for years to come."
Oscar Hernández, pianist with Rubén Blades – "An excellent and much needed resource."

The Brazilian Guitar Book

By Nelson Faria, one of Brazil's best new guitarists.

- Over 140 pages of comping patterns, transcriptions and chord melodies for samba, bossa, baião, etc.
- Complete chord voicings written out for each example.
- Comes with a CD of Nelson playing each example.
- The most complete Brazilian guitar method ever published! $28.

Joe Diorio – "Nelson Faria's book is a welcome addition to the guitar literature. I'm sure those who work with this volume wiill benefit greatly"

Inside The Brazilian Rhythm Section
By Nelson Faria and Cliff Korman

This is the first book/CD package ever published that provides an opportunity for bassists, guitarists, pianists and drummers to interact and play-along with a master Brazilian rhythm section. Perfect for practicing both accompanying and soloing.

$28 list price for book and 2 CDs - including the charts for the CD tracks and sample parts for each instrument, transcribed from the recording.

The Latin Bass Book
A PRACTICAL GUIDE
By Oscar Stagnaro

The only comprehensive book ever published on how to play bass in authentic Afro-Cuban, Brazilian, Caribbean, Latin Jazz & South American styles. $34.

Over 250 pages of transcriptions of Oscar Stagnaro playing each exercise. Learn from the best!

Includes: 3 Play-Along CDs to accompany each exercise, featuring world-class rhythm sections.

Afro-Caribbean Grooves for Drumset

By Jean-Philippe Fanfant, drummer with Andy narell's band, Sakesho.

Covers grooves from 10 Caribbean nations, arranged for drumset.

Endorsed by Peter Erskine, Horacio Hernandez, etc.

CD includes both audio and video files. $25.

The Digital Real Book

On the web

Over 850 downloadable tunes from all the Sher Music Co. fakebooks.

See www.shermusic.com for details.

Foundation Exercises for Bass

By Chuck Sher

A creative approach for any style of music, any level, acoustic or electric bass. Perfect for bass teachers!

Filled with hundreds of exercises to help you master scales, chords, rhythms, hand positions, ear training, reading music, sample bass grooves, creating bass lines on common chord progressions, and much more.

$24

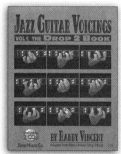

Jazz Guitar Voicings The Drop 2 Book

By Randy Vincent, Everything you need to know to create full chord melody voicings like Jim Hall, Joe Pass, etc. Luscious voicings for chord melody playing based on the "Drop 2" principle of chord voicings.

You will find that this book covers this essential material in a unique way unlike any other guitar book available.

Endorsed by Julian Lage, John Stowell, Larry Koonse, etc.

$25, includes 2 CDs.

Walking Bassics: The Fundamentals of Jazz Bass Playing

By swinging NY bassist Ed Fuqua

Includes transcriptions of every bass note on accompanying CD and step-by-step method for constructing solid walking bass lines. $22.

Endorsed by Eddie Gomez, Jimmy Haslip, John Goldsby, etc.

Three-Note Voicings and Beyond

By Randy Vincent, A complete guide to the construction and use of every kind of three-note voicing on guitar.

"Randy Vincent is an extraordinary musician. This book illuminates harmonies in the most sensible and transparent way." – **Pat Metheny**

"This book is full of essential information for jazz guitarists at any level. Wonderful!" – **Mike Stern**

194 pages, $28

Concepts for Bass Soloing

By Chuck Sher and Marc Johnson, (bassist with Bill Evans, etc.) The only book ever published that is specifically designed to improve your soloing! $26

- Includes two CDs of Marc Johnson soloing on each exercise
- Transcriptions of bass solos by: Eddie Gomez, John Patitucci, Scott LaFaro, Jimmy Haslip, etc.

"It's a pleasure to encounter a Bass Method so well conceived and executed." – **Steve Swallow**

The Jazz Piano Book

By Mark Levine, Concord recording artist and pianist with Cal Tjader. For beginning to advanced pianists. The only truly comprehensive method ever published! Over 300 pages. $32
Richie Beirach – "The best new method book available."
Hal Galper – "This is a must!"
Jamey Aebersold – "This is an invaluable resource for any pianist."
James Williams – "One of the most complete anthologies on jazz piano."
Also available in Spanish! ¡El Libro del Jazz Piano!

The Improvisor's Bass Method

By Chuck Sher. A complete method for electric or acoustic bass, plus transcribed solos and bass lines by Mingus, Jaco, Ron Carter, Scott LaFaro, Paul Jackson, Ray Brown, and more! Over 200 pages. $16

International Society of Bassists – "Undoubtedly the finest book of its kind."
Eddie Gomez – "Informative, readily comprehensible and highly imaginative"

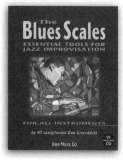

The Blues Scales

ESSENTIAL TOOLS FOR JAZZ IMPROVISATION
By Dan Greenblatt

Great Transcriptions from Miles, Dizzy Gillespie, Lester Young, Oscar Peterson, Dave Sanborn, Michael Brecker and many more, showing how the Blues Scales are actually used in various styles of jazz.

Accompanying CD by author Dan Greenblatt and his swinging quartet of New York jazz musicians shows how each exercise should sound. And it also gives the student numerous play-along tracks to practice with. $22

Essential Grooves

FOR WRITING, PERFORMING AND PRODUCING CONTEMPORARY MUSIC
By 3 Berklee College professors: Dan Moretti, Matthew Nicholl and Oscar Stagnaro

- 41 different rhythm section grooves used in Soul, Rock, Motown, Funk, Hip-hop, Jazz, Afro-Cuban, Brazilian, music and more!
- Includes CD and multi-track DVD with audio files to create play-alongs, loops, original music, and more.

$24

Forward Motion

FROM BACH TO BEBOP
A Corrective Approach to Jazz Phrasing
By Hal Galper

- Perhaps the most important jazz book in a decade, Foward Motion shows the reader how to create jazz phrases that swing with authentic jazz feeling.
- Hal Galper was pianist with Cannonball Adderley, Phil Woods, Stan Getz, Chet Baker, John Scofield, and many other jazz legends.
- Each exercise available on an interactive website so that the reader can change tempos, loop the exercises, transpose them, etc. $30.

The World's Greatest Fake Book

Jazz & Fusion Tunes by: **Coltrane, Mingus, Jaco, Chick Corea, Bird, Herbie Hancock, Bill Evans, McCoy, Beirach, Ornette, Wayne Shorter, Zawinul, AND MANY MORE!** $32

Chick Corea – "Great for any students of jazz.'
Dave Liebman – "The fake book of the 80's."
George Cables – "The most carefully conceived fake book I've ever seen."